MW00781270

"As a patternmaker and product developer who has worked with many startups over the years, I have been so impressed with Mindy's program and how prepared her students are for the realities of the industry. Everything from the order in which tasks need to be accomplished, to the importance of identifying and always coming back to the target consumer, how to communicate effectively with vendors, factories and service providers, and setting the expectations for the prototyping process. Mindy is a trusted guide who presents information in an approachable way, yet doesn't sugarcoat the fact that starting a business in fashion isn't easy. She helps to navigate through the nuances and noise so entrepreneurs who follow the program have a big advantage over their competition."

—XOCHIL HERRERA SCHEER, Apparel Engineer;
Product Development Expert; Owner, The Chicago Pattern Maker

"In an industry that has been ravaged by offshoring, Mindy recognized what most others have not and seized upon the opportunities to gain competitive advantages within domestic sourcing. Building upon her vast industry experience, she built a thriving manufacturing business that leverages those advantages and supporting the Made in America movement. In addition to her success in sewn products manufacturing, she has expanded her influence upon the industry through education and teaching aspiring apparel entrepreneurs to understand the industry and how to succeed as a domestic brand. Her immeasurable impact upon this industry is undeniable and limitless. Mindy truly is a shining star!

"Now Mindy has taken her vast knowledge and experience in a convoluted industry and turned it into this book. This is a valuable resource to any apparel entrepreneur and clothing designer. From honing an initial design concept to selecting manufacturers, this book [Mindy] walks you through the real-world steps."

—WILL DUNCAN, Executive Director, SEAMS;
The Association & Voice of the US sewn products industry

"The Apparel Mentor has been invaluable to my journey as a fashion entrepreneur. Mindy and her team have provided guidance, support, detailed and practical advice and resources, and—most importantly—the needed courage and encouragement to keep the entire process from development to launch moving along. The decades of experience this team shares with program participants has allowed me to feel confident and supported in an industry where I have zero prior experience. Our monthly mentor meetings, quick feedback from the team on issues and questions encountered along the way, and support and collaboration of the community of participants are the reason I am still on this journey of fashion entrepreneurship. I highly recommend this book and program to anyone thinking about or engaged in fashion entrepreneurship!"

—PAIGE ROBERTS, Apparel Mentor Member and Accessory Brand Owner

"The Apparel Mentor brought me from a woman with an idea to a confident soon-to-be-manufacturer. Mindy gave me an entire framework for manufacturing, . . . piece by digestible piece. Each week is a lesson and assignment, doable because it builds on the last one. Starting with my mission (which was critiqued in class until it was substantive and essential), I determined fabric, reached out to vendors, started working with a pattern maker, and created my first prototypes . . . all within our lesson plan. Wanting to be prepared for my next class pushed me outside my comfort zone, to do what I'd been coached to do: prepare samples, call textile mills and factories, attend trade shows. I learned to reasonably estimate costs and determine price of finished product. Thanks to Apparel Mentor [Mindy], I have an educated manufacturing timeline that will soon be leading to my first sales. I strongly recommend taking the step to enroll in Apparel Mentor if the one thing you are missing is an informed plan."

—SHEVON DIETERICH, Owner, She Threds; Apparel Mentor Member

GET IT MADE

BUILD YOUR **CLOTHING LINE**
FROM **IDEA** TO **REALITY**

The
Apparel Mentor
MINDY MARTELL

Published by

MANDALA TREE PRESS
mandalatreepress.com

First Printing 2023

Paperback ISBN: 9781954801523
Hardcover with Dust Jacket ISBN: 9781954801516
Case Laminate Hardcover ISBN: 9781954801509
eBook ISBN: 9781954801530

BUS070090	BUSINESS & ECONOMICS / Industries / Fashion & Textile Industry
DES005000	DESIGN / Fashion & Accessories
TEC040000	TECHNOLOGY & ENGINEERING / Technical & Manufacturing Industries & Trades

Cover design and typesetting by Kaitlin Barwick
Edited by Emily Chambers

theapparelmentor.com

To my mother, Patricia, and my grandmother, Anne. Your bottomless wells of patience and teaching all throughout my life have made me who I am today.

CONTENTS

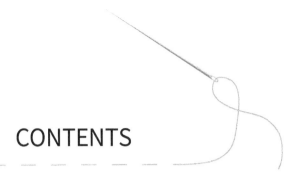

SECTION 2
FIND YOUR FABRIC | 79

SECTION 3
DEVELOP YOUR SAMPLES | 115

SECTION 4
CREATE TECH PACK & SIZING | 169

SECTION 5
SELECT YOUR FACTORY | 225

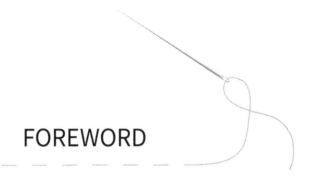

FOREWORD

In an industry that has been ravaged by offshoring, Mindy recognized what most others have not and seized upon the opportunities to gain competitive advantages within domestic sourcing. Building upon her vast industry experience, she built a thriving manufacturing business that leverages those advantages and supports the Made in America movement.

In addition to her success in sewn products manufacturing, she has expanded her influence upon the industry through education and teaching aspiring apparel entrepreneurs to understand the industry and how to succeed as a domestic brand. Her immeasurable impact upon this industry is undeniable and limitless. Mindy truly is a shining star!

Now Mindy has taken her vast knowledge and experience in a convoluted industry and turned it into this book. This is a valuable resource to any apparel entrepreneurs and clothing designers. From honing an initial design concept to selecting manufacturers, this book walks you through the real-world steps.

WILL DUNCAN

Executive Director, SEAMS
The Association & Voice of the US sewn products industry

INTRODUCTION

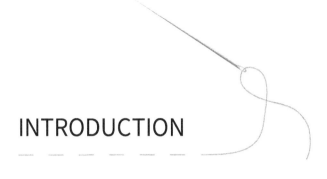

Welcome. I'm so glad you're here. First off, let me commend you for wanting to launch your own apparel line—and for taking the necessary steps to get there. As a small business owner with a dream, you are the future of the apparel industry I've loved for twenty years. Helping people like you break into this world has become my life's work. My purpose in this book is to do just that.

I'm Mindy Martell, president and founder of two separate companies: Clothier Design Source and The Apparel Mentor. I've devoted my career to helping designers like you. I've been in this industry since 2000, and I founded my own development house and factory in 2008. Since that time, I've helped more than one thousand new clothing brands make hundreds of thousands of products.

I started Clothier Design Source, the factory, because nobody was there to help me when I was in your position. I had to figure things out myself. Over the years, I grew tired of seeing the same scene play out, over and over again: A new clothing brand would come up with an idea, an audience, and a plan. But as soon as they tried to manufacture their product, the old-school factories wouldn't give them the time of day. It happened to me, and I saw it happening all around me.

Even back then, I *knew* these brands could succeed, but to make things work, they needed more attention, more education, more help. So I decided to step in and apply my expertise to the problem. Since that time, my company and I have worked hard to prove that small businesses deserve a spot at the table. But that's not enough. Now, we need to shape the future of this industry. Of course, that can't happen if we keep things the way they are. Underground networks need to be replaced with transparency. Confusion needs to be replaced with education. Roles that have been undervalued need to claim the respect they deserve.

WHY I WROTE THIS BOOK

For years I've wanted to write this book. I can't tell you how many times I've wished I could hand someone a step-by-step guide to the tips and tricks that live in my head. Now that it's finally materialized, let me explain why I think that those tips and tricks are valuable.

In the past, some designers have told me they're drawn to my experience or passion. I love hearing that! Those are important characteristics, and I'm committed to showing them to you. But if you ask me, there's another reason I hope you want to read this book: I *love* teaching. For me, it's not enough to know the mechanics of this industry. I truly want to help you. I love showing others what I've learned and helping them achieve their own dreams. And I'm invested in your success.

THE APPAREL MENTOR

For a long time, I approached both aspects of my work under the same business umbrella: I ran a factory to produce apparel products and new clothing brands, and I educated and guided people through the same process I went through. But by 2017, I realized that I needed to separate these two aspects of my business—because the need for education in the fashion and apparel industry is *so big*. There's so much about this industry that's incomprehensible to anyone who doesn't have decades of experience working in it.

I *do* have that experience, and I'm passionate about sharing it to help others, so I started The Apparel Mentor to dedicate myself to guiding individuals who want to produce their own new clothing brands. This book is the natural result of that shift: a collection of step-by-step lessons, strategies, and warnings cultivated from my insider's experience in the industry.

With The Apparel Mentor, which is an educational and mentoring company, I have developed systems and processes and tools that I can give directly to people and to other mentors in order to improve the chances for success of different new clothing brands throughout the United States. The whole purpose is to teach individuals, startups, and entrepreneurs to grow the community at the ground level.

That's who I am. So, what about you? Perhaps creativity is what draws you to the apparel industry. You see features that clothes *should* have, but for now they exist only in your mind. Maybe your business acumen brought you here. As an established business owner, you know how to leverage opportunity in your marketplace, but you're brand new to the apparel industry. Or maybe you tried to find clothing that meets your needs, but got frustrated because nobody's making it. Not yet, anyway!

As for me, I followed a long and winding road to get here myself. Some people might see my success in the industry today and assume that I always knew I wanted to work in fashion and that I've had top-quality education and training to get me here. But that's not really the case at all.

A BIT ABOUT ME AND HOW I GOT HERE

I grew up in rural Minnesota. My grandma lived with us, and she taught me how to sew, so I grew up doing a lot of sewing projects just for fun. I was making a lot of doll clothes, my own clothes, gifts for friends and family—stuff like that. When I was old enough, I went to college—for something completely different at first. I fell into a new routine there where I'd go to class, go to my job, and then come home to sew and design in my spare time—again, just as a hobby. My then-boyfriend, now-husband saw how I lived on a daily basis and said something to the effect of "Hey, it seems like you really love sewing. So why aren't you going to school for that?"

That had honestly never occurred to me! His comments ended up changing my whole direction in life. I switched to a tech school where I could study apparel manufacturing, and I just ate it up. I absolutely loved it. I interned for a while in the industry and worked a few different jobs to get experience: domestic production for a small men's underwear company, head developer for women's wear, and on and on.

After I had kids, I decided I wanted more flexibility, and I transitioned into freelance designing. Frankly, that's when this whole monstrosity was born—the urge to help others, establishing a program and a whole company designed to enable others to build their own new clothing brands, and even this book itself.

I didn't have a particularly well thought-out plan before I started—I didn't know this is what I wanted to do from day one. I found myself moving from one project to the next, one goal to the next, and then, years later, I was in a position to help others move along the same process—but hopefully much more easily. So it's okay if you don't have it all figured out ahead of time, or if your motivations for starting your own apparel line are uniquely yours. That's great! Whatever your inspiration, I'm here to help.

HOW I CAN HELP YOU

Whatever your reasons for being here, no matter what brought you here, you were on my mind as I wrote this book. Time and time again, I've seen new clothing brands realize too late that this industry isn't set up for them. Instead, it was built by and for big companies. It's survived for decades on a model that's set in its ways, even when it should be adapting faster to today's marketplace. If you dive into the current system as a new clothing brand, no matter your creativity or business acumen, you'll find significant roadblocks and challenges. I've experienced those obstacles, and developed ways to help you overcome them.

Even though you're the future, the apparel industry hasn't caught up with you yet. Many of its infrastructures exist underground, and knowledge is reserved for those who already know the system. If you're a new clothing brand, very few people who are already in that system are willing or able to show you the ropes. You need to know what you're walking into. This industry isn't built for you, and it doesn't work the way it ought to—and that means you could fail no matter how great your idea might be. (And many new clothing brands do.) This guide exists because I want to see you succeed—and I'm going to tell you everything you need to know.

I wrote this book because I want to help you bridge that gap between talent and success. I want to share what I learned from my own experiences so that yours are smoother and more successful. I want to help answer some of those questions up front—or at least point you in the right direction to save valuable time. I look forward to guiding you step-by-step through the journey that lies before you. Whether you're at the planning stage or are already in process, here's how I can help.

WHO THIS BOOK IS FOR

This book is for you if:

- You've been dreaming about starting an apparel line, but don't know where to start.
- You've taken steps to start your clothing company, but realized this industry is tougher to break into than you thought.
- You've already established your own small clothing business, but you did it through the school of hard knocks. This time, you're ready to be savvier about your time, money, and effort.

WHAT THIS BOOK IS

- A step-by-step process for new clothing brands launching an apparel line.

- A no-nonsense guide to an industry that can be unkind to new, small brands.
- A how-to for becoming a brand manager who oversees countless decisions and interactions with industry vendors.
- A strategic reminder to manage your resources—time, energy, and money—as you go.
- A collection of stories, insights, and testimonials outlining paths to success for new clothing brands.
- An enthusiastic champion for you and your business! You are the future of this industry.

WHAT THIS BOOK ISN'T

- A how-to for pattern making or the art of garment design.
- A deep dive into the logistics of running a business.
- A guide to marketing, inventory, and everything that comes after launching your line.
- A magic fairy guaranteeing that your clothing will appear easily and perfectly. This process takes resources and grit, but the rewards are worth it.

WHAT YOU NEED TO GET STARTED

Every business is different. Every designer has their own goals. Only you know how many resources are available to you in terms of time, energy, and finances. Maybe you'll hire a design house to manage your projects; maybe you'll work entirely in DIY mode. A designer who can work full-time on this endeavor will finish faster than a side-gig warrior creating a passion project.

I started from scratch. You've got this book, as well as a host of other tools available to you, so you can rest assured that at least the road will be a little easier for you.

I had a lot of experience in the industry when I started working on my own products for my own new clothing brand, but even I didn't jump into the process with everything figured out or with all my resources, contacts, and plans laid out for me. I started building my work piece by piece. In the beginning, when my clientele grew beyond my own schedule, I hired a couple of people to work out of my house with me and help out. At this point, we were just designing and finding factories to handle manufacturing and then managing the workload through those factories. My husband and I had our dining room table set up on paint cans so it was high enough for us to stand and cut fabric. We'd lay out the fabric on the table as we were working on our designs.

Yes, I'd graduated design school and worked in the industry for several different companies—but I was still hiring my friends to sew in my living room. Like so many other designers I ended up working with, the story was the same: you graduate, you have this degree, and you are still completely confused about how the industry works. There's something missing in the education system. They teach you how to make a pattern, how to fit a garment, all those technical details—but the industry side is missing the practical details you need to know to actually make your designs a reality.

When I left design school, I was just as confused. I knew how to make a pretty garment—one of them. But how to make thousands? How to work with the interconnected industry, with fiber and fabric mills, with trim providers, with cutting and sewing factories? I had no idea how any of that worked.

Design schools are great for teaching you designs. But they don't give you any practical, real-world, hands-on knowledge for succeeding in the industry.

And that's the purpose of this book. Passion, good ideas, talent, hard work—all of those are vital, but even together, they're not always enough for success, because the *industry isn't built for what you want to accomplish.* You have to wrangle it into shape to make it work for you. And in this book, I've collected the lessons and guidelines to help you get there.

So back to the initial question—what do you need to get started? Well, everything I've just listed—passion, good ideas, talent, hard work, and this book—is a pretty good start. And I'm willing to bet you've got the necessary traits to get going, because you're reading this book and you're taking steps to do things right, to learn what you need to know.

As for the specific resources, processes, and collaborators you'll need? All approaches are equally valid, so I'm asking you to *play your own game.* It's easy to compare yourself to so-and-so you see on social media who's living the designer's life you've been envisioning. But all that matters is you, your project, and—ultimately—your customers.

HOW MUCH DOES IT COST TO LAUNCH A LINE?

Just as I can't tell you how long your line will take to produce, there's no way I can predict your ultimate expenses. Think of this as building a house. Nobody would approach an architect cold and say, "I want to build a house. How much will it cost?" This individual is sure to respond with a gazillion questions about what kind of house you want. Tiny house or mansion? Eco-friendly or budget-conscious? What specialty materials are involved? On and on, the questions must go, until everyone has a shared understanding or what they're working with.

But let me help you get some of that shared understanding up front so you know what kinds of factors and commonalities to consider.

- Manufacturing a garment requires anywhere from five to fifteen vendors. You may have heard about patternmakers and sewers, but this book will introduce you to other specialists you'll need.
- When manufacturing, there is an economy of scale. To make it worthwhile to work with a factory, a designer may want to produce at least 300 garments.
- To meet the needs of a marketplace, a clothing line may need five sizes in its first run. This, combined with the number of styles to make, influences your cost estimate.
- There are two major categories of costs: materials and labor. By labor, I'm referring to all the steps covered in this book, from hiring your first tech designer to having the factory ship your final garment. When it comes to labor—again, all the steps covered in this book—you should expect to spend a minimum of $8,000 to $10,000. These costs will come in pieces, in steps that you control, over the course of your entire process.
- Material costs vary widely and can't be predicted in this setting.

These are just reference points. Like everything in this book—like everything in this *industry*—there are no hard-and-fast rules, no magic wands, no guarantees. But setting yourself up with realistic plans, sufficient timetables, and the right mindset will prime you for success in launching your new clothing brand. I want you to be well equipped to tackle whatever challenges you might face, and that includes having the appropriate expectations and information from the outset.

DO YOU HAVE WHAT IT TAKES?

I'm a believer in spending our time on things that matter most. Anything worth doing takes time and effort, and a strong sense of purpose should be our guide. When I meet aspiring designers, I like to ask them *why* they want to do it. Are they a hobby sewist who discovered a hot market? Are they a fashion-school grad who has been envisioning this path for years? Did they stumble into this industry, after seeing a business opportunity from another venture?

All of these are equally viable reasons to start a clothing line. I've seen countless successes from every one of these approaches, and more. That said, I've also observed that there *are* better times than others to start an apparel line. When you take on this process, it's ideal for you to be ready to take on the tasks of a project manager. You'll fare better if you're ready to communicate proactively, oversee details, hire vendors, and learn many lessons along the way.

If this sounds like you right now, let's go!! I can't wait to get you started. Seeing your design come to life, then reach your customers' hands, is an exciting journey. Alternatively, you may have picked up this book to prepare yourself for down the road. If this is your case, I commend you. Kudos to you for taking the time to learn about the process. Deciding to prepare for a future launch by educating yourself now is just as necessary a step as creating that first design or reaching out to that first vendor. By reading this book, you should be able to avoid many of the pitfalls that are easy for new designers to make.

JUST BECAUSE YOU BUILD IT, DOESN'T MEAN THEY'LL COME

Speaking of pitfalls, I'll share a big one with you right now. Time and time again, I've seen new designers get so excited about their line that they forget to pay attention to other parts of running a business. I get it. When you've dreamed of producing your own clothes for years, then spent months getting those clothes to the factory, it can be hard to believe that people won't immediately rush to buy your fantastic product.

But here's the thing: People won't buy your clothes if they don't know they exist. Trust me when I tell you that *it does not matter how gorgeous and functional and comfortable your pieces are.* Your clothes won't sell without an effective marketing plan. Period. The same goes for your business operations. Without solid, thoughtful operations designed to handle all aspects of your product, you won't reach any of your potential customers. As you develop your design, start thinking about how you'll build structures for fundamentals like inventory management, customer service, and legal policies.

Indeed, producing wonderful clothing is just part of the equation. Of course, it's an incredibly important and satisfying part, which is why I'm devoting this book to it. But before you dig in, I want to set the context for what you can expect from this process. I'm already invested in your success. I want you to have all the tools you need for an effective, successful, and meaningful new clothing brand launch. My hope is that you'll do better, the more you know.

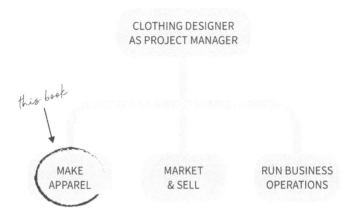

HOW TO USE THIS BOOK

First and foremost, this book is designed for action. My goal is to provide you with the right information to move from idea to launch. As such, every chapter is accompanied by digital **worksheets** that walk you through the tasks you should execute at this step. Look for the prompts throughout that lead you to the numbered worksheets, which you have free access to with your purchase of this book.

Each lesson is here for a reason. I've included stories from my own experiences in the industry, particularly those experiences that have taught me valuable lessons about what to avoid in future endeavors. I've written about these lessons to help you avoid the pitfalls I've seen hundreds of other designers encounter over the years. These pitfalls can be costly and highly frustrating, so *I strongly encourage you to complete every lesson in the book.*

I recognize that some of you may be in process already, so you'll need to start in the middle. If this is the case for you, that's okay. Start where you need to now. Then, when it comes time to develop your *next* line, start from the beginning of the book.

On the other hand, some of you will start from the beginning. Wonderful! You have the opportunity to avoid some challenges you may not have seen coming. Even so, you may get tempted, from time to time, to skip a step. I fully understand that temptation—the urge to jump ahead into the next phase of product launch, to get to the really good stuff. But no matter where you start, I implore you to finish every lesson, especially if you value your sanity, your money, or both.

Though each lesson is important, it's up to you to take ownership of *how* you complete them. I encourage you to make this book your own. I've provided you with a structure to follow, but you get to make it come alive in a way that works for you and your brand. If you need to revisit a lesson or fill out a worksheet more than once, do it! If you need to slow down the process or speed it up, do what works for you. Decide how large your team should be, how sparse or fancy you want your garment to be, and how to manage your resources as you go. I suggest you use the QR code below now to print out the full workbook and put in a binder so you can work along with the book. We will have prompts throughout the book when to go back to the workbook.

TO WORK ALONG WITH THIS BOOK,
USE THIS QR CODE TO PRINT THE
ENTIRE **WORKBOOK** NOW.

WHAT ARE THE REWARDS?

Oh, you guys. I'm thrilled to be able to share with you a path to one of the most rewarding tasks I know: Putting your *very own* clothing line into the world brings so many rewards. So. Many. Rewards.

Let me tell you a few brief stories about designers who've changed the lives of dozens of people—themselves, their families, or their communities. The names involved here have been changed, but the stories are true and the rewards are things I've seen firsthand. I'll walk you through brief backstories for these designers so you understand that the rewards of producing your own clothing line are available to all kinds of people.

NORDIC FASHION

First, we've got a brand we'll call Nordic Fashion. This is a company led by somebody we'll call Jack, who worked in a completely different industry, Olympic skiing, with his own clients and business. Jack realized that one of his problems could be solved by developing a cut and sew product. Jack really knew his stuff when it came to skiing. He recognized that there was a problem that wasn't being met by the products available to him at the time.

Jack had the idea for the solution, but there was one problem—Jack didn't know jack about the apparel industry (pun intended). He wanted something that looked good and was comfortable, but he didn't know how to get started on it. He needed a partner because he literally didn't know anything about the industry. Why would he? He didn't even know how to talk about stitches. So he called me up and became a client, and we got started. We collaborated, and I walked him through the process pretty much as outlined in this book. We made his idea a reality—a very successful one.

This was in 2008 or 2009, and Jack—and Nordic Fashion—have remained part of what we do every week since then. We still manufacture products in our factories for him constantly. Flat out, he's changed the industry. He's completely revolutionized apparel for Olympic and competitive skiers. All it took was a good idea on his part—and the follow through to find a partner that would work with him in order to make it a reality.

The rewards in this case are obvious. Jack got the products he needed and has been able to help his athletes perform better. He's changed his whole field. For us, we had the chance to work with a great client and see their creativity realized. This is just one example of the rewards of putting your own clothing line out into the world.

BABIES UNLIMITED

Now let me talk about Babies Unlimited, another client and brand I work with. Babies Unlimited was my very first manufacturing client, and I'm still producing their products literally as I'm writing this. They've been with us since 2006. I was cutting their designs and fabrics in my kitchen when I first started out.

Just like with Nordic Fashion, Babies Unlimited wasn't started by someone in the apparel industry. This is an organization with people who had a great idea for products and wanted to make them a reality. Their product was backed by scientific studies and was designed to help monitor the growth and development of children.

Pretty amazing, right? The only problem was that they had this awesome device and they didn't know how to attach it to an infant's body in a way that was comfortable and, you know, nonflammable and safe. Those little important details when you're working with kids can be overwhelming.

So we started working with Babies Unlimited. We got their product made safely and efficiently. Our collaborations worked—and they still continue today, because Babies Unlimited has been incredibly successful. Their products have had a major impact on improving families' lives and child rearing throughout the country.

HUNTING APPAREL

The rewards for starting your own clothing line are as endless and varied as the types of clothing you might dream up. I've worked with a client who's producing a hunting brand. Hunting clothes have to be incredibly functional, of course, but our client has focused on marketing to people who *also* care that their clothing is made in the United States, which is a big deal for us. This was a pet project for him—he didn't know anything about apparel, but he had an interest and a passion and saw a way that he could solve a problem—and now he's meeting a specific demand in the market.

HEALTH WORKER GEAR

We're working with another client that's making headwear for nurses. She recognized that nurses have a specific problem with their hair when they're at work, so she designed a product—a really *cute* product, I should add—to solve it. Her products are now in literally every hospital in the United States.

These are just a few of the clients we've worked with who have seen amazing success. Their products are different, their personalities are different, their approaches are different, and they've all seen the rewards firsthand of making this work. They've followed my lessons and advice, we've worked hard together, and they've achieved their goals and more.

WHY I DO WHAT I DO

Helping people like those outlined above is what rewards and motivates me. The things that drive me in my work have changed over time. For a while, I was focused on just getting my own designs out there into the world. Later, I really wanted to help demystify the apparel industry and guide others past the pitfalls I'd encountered in my own work. Now, however, I've been focused a lot more on systemic issues in the apparel industry. This isn't something I necessarily set out to tackle from the beginning, but it's been a deeply satisfying aspect of my work over time, and my mission and focus have adapted to suit my developing interests.

My feminism drives me. My desire to empower and enable women to achieve their dreams drives me. I'm focused on trying to help get the apparel design industry standardized and taken more seriously around the world—and especially in the United States. The industry is 80% run by women. Well, I should say: 80% of the *work* is done by women. The reality is that the industry is largely run by men. That's a big deal to me—I want to help equalize things, make sure that women are getting the chances and the recognition they deserve for their hard work. That's a *huge* motivator and reward for something that started as living room freelance designing and sewing!

More than that, I want to make sure products in the industry are ethically made. That's another big driver for me. The ethical production of clothing worldwide is a major problem. In many countries, workers are paid something like a penny a day for often grueling work—that's a form of servitude, slavery even. It's unethical. It's not something I can change single-handed, but I've worked to make a little dent in the problem by focusing on U.S.-based manufacturing. Labor laws in the United States mean that I can feel like I'm making a difference with every piece of clothing that I help make here. These are little victories, sure, but they're incredibly rewarding to me personally.

Those are just a few of the rewards I've seen for my own work in the industry, and they're the reason I wrote this book to help you. Whatever you're looking for, whatever you're hoping to get out of this endeavor, I think you'll find that you're surprised by how rewarding and satisfied the journey and the end results are.

All right, you've gotten a glimpse of the big picture. You know this work isn't going to be easy, but you see the possibilities of how it can change your life. You want to make your future customers happy and take an active role in reshaping the apparel industry.

Are you getting excited yet? Are you a little bit nervous? It's all part of this fulfilling, wonderful process. And if at this point you're already thinking to yourself that this is more than you feel you can tackle on your own, or you can tell you'll need more accountability and personalized coaching, feel free to reach out to me at theapparelmentor.com. Otherwise, when you're ready to read on, let's get started!

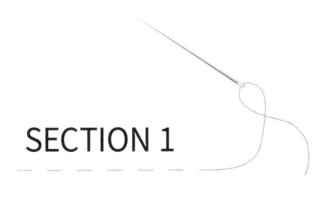

SECTION 1

DEFINE YOUR DESIGN

In this section, you will do all the preplanning that is needed to have a successful development process. The more defining and planning you do, the more successful you will be!

LESSON 1

DEFINE YOUR MISSION

Lesson Objectives

In this lesson, you will:

- ▶ Name your company.
- ▶ Write or revisit your mission statement in one to two sentences.
- ▶ Set your five to seven core values.
- ▶ Find out who your competitors are.
- ▶ Describe what makes your brand different.
- ▶ Identify an inspiration brand.

PRINT AND SAVE THIS **MANUFACTURING CHECKLIST** FOR AN OVERVIEW OF WHAT WE WILL BE WORKING ON THROUGHOUT THIS BOOK.

If I had a chance to talk with you one on one, there is one main piece of information I would be after: *Why do you want to make a clothing line?* I've heard countless stories about what motivates people to bring their own apparel line into the world. The ones who answer with a unique reason and story are the ones that excite me. It all starts with you having a clear vision and a clear "why." Your answer would tell me so much. It would tell me what matters to you. It would tell me who your customers are and how your garments will stand out. Not only that, but your answer may even give me a sense for what your development process will turn out like.

— — Mentor Moment — —

I know I just said that the people with a unique reason and story are the ones that excite me, but that doesn't mean you have to have everything figured out from the very beginning. I didn't! I have a very clear, precise mission now that allows me to achieve what I'm really focused on, but it definitely didn't start that way.

I come from a labor-heavy background. When I was young, my dad worked away from home, and my mom stayed home to take care of us and raise our chickens and grow our garden. We all worked, and it was pretty mundane, dirty work at that. I had a pretty normal life with pretty normal work experience in that regard. At that point in my life, it would have seemed too lofty or glamorous or unreal to think that I might have a job designing clothes, of all things. For us, working at a job was a means to an end, something simple and straightforward for a result—not very creative, usually.

So it didn't really occur to me for a long time that I could actually get a job as a designer, that I could make my work something that fulfilled a personal mission and satisfied me creatively and allowed me to help others. It seems obvious in retrospect, but it took me years to get to that point. I think it just might have seemed self-indulgent back then—before I realized all of the really hard work it does involve.

I've already mentioned that at college I was majoring in something *other* than designing for a while. I was pursuing Asian Studies and the Mandarin language. It wasn't that I didn't have big ambitions—the opposite, honestly, though it's a little silly to look back on. World trade had really exploded at that point under the Bush administration, and I knew manufacturing was going to be huge in the coming years, especially in China. Even then I knew I was going to be involved in that whole process. I'm not sure what I was expecting—maybe that I was going to be in the importing business with China, since I was studying Asian culture and Mandarin. I didn't really have a defined mission, I suppose, but I knew I wanted to work hard and be involved and make something.

When I eventually realized that I could actually work in the fashion industry as a designer, I had to abandon the Asian studies major and transfer to a local tech college for two years. After that, my first real job in the industry was an internship working as a pattern maker and pre-production coordinator. I was at a really little company that basically just hired me as an intern and gave me way too much responsibility. And that was great for me! I learned a ton in that role (particularly about men's underwear), and I had some good hands-on experience working with factories and vendors and the rest.

But here's the part that really led to understanding my own mission—the culmination of this part of my story demonstrates how recognizing your reasons for being involved in making your own clothing line is a vital step in your journey. Yes, I got some great hands-on experience working as an intern, but I also saw firsthand how complicated, muddled, confusing, and overwhelming the whole system already was. This company had been around for about twelve years before I started working there. They had at least twelve years of experience in the industry—and things were still a mess! They were using cottage industry approaches in their work. They'd manage to get through the design process (I'm still not sure exactly how) and then reach out to various sewing groups and the like to get their samples made. It was rocky and challenging, and it really opened my eyes to the huge gap in resources available to people wanting to make their own clothes available to the public.

Those experiences really set me on my current path. I recognized a problem in the industry and saw a way that I might

LESSON 1: DEFINE YOUR MISSION

be able to help fix it. Later, when my second son was born in 2007, I told the company I was working for that I wanted to scale down to part time to be at home more and have more flexibility in my work. That's when I really started being able to build my freelance business at home.

Of course, because it's kind of my go-to thing to turn something flexible into something much *less* flexible, I started up a business at home, hiring people to help me, reaching out to people online, focusing all my efforts on laying the ground-work for other people who were trying to break into the apparel industry. And then I was smack in the middle of the hurricane trying to address the problems I'd been seeing for years.

Looking back, there was never a concrete moment when I decided to start a business helping people establish their own new clothing brands and clothing lines. It was completely an organic process, as I've just described. And yet, from these experiences and the development of my interests regarding clothing manufacturing, my own mission has become clear.

So yes, I want you to figure out your mission, your why, and your purpose and focus. But I recognize that getting there can take a lot of time. It might not immediately be clear what your mission is, so give it some deep, honest thought.

――― ―― ―― ――

Your "why" matters, *a lot.* This is true of any business venture, but it's critically important for new clothing brands. Having a clear understanding of your brand's "why" can make or break your success. One simple reason is it's very difficult to know when you've met your goals if you don't understand why you're trying to reach them, or what success really looks like. You can't get where you're going if you don't have a good idea of what it looks like, or why you're getting started. And changing your motivation can drastically change your ideas of success as well.

Another reason the "why" matters so much is that the market for fashion products has drastically changed in recent years. In today's economy, we live in a world of niches. This is a major shift from the mass markets that drove economic success decades ago. Thanks to ever-changing forces like accessible technology and increasing global awareness, small business owners now have new ways to reach *their* people, and vice versa.

New clothing brands have an opportunity to serve a narrow but loyal target market. Products that may not have been available in a mass market for the mainstream now have a chance to thrive. For example, Amira is a startup in my hometown of Twin Cities, Minnesota, that makes sports hijabs. Their tagline is "Modest Activewear," and their site reads, "Still today Muslim girls don't have options for culturally appropriate activewear." What other niche apparel companies come to mind?

One thing I want you to keep in mind is that the exigencies of the marketplace have some limitations on how you can find success with your new clothing brand. But these limitations aren't inherently a bad thing. In fact, they will force you to innovate, to find a mission that speaks to you, and to reach a niche clientele that truly appreciates your products.

One of the hardest things to realize in this industry is that people who just want to make pretty things *simply aren't successful.* If you're like, "Oh my gosh, I want to make a really pretty skirt and sell it to people," unfortunately, you're very unlikely to find any success with that. That's a really common sentiment for people who want to get into the fashion industry—they want to be known for designing the hottest dresses or the most flattering, adorable pants you've ever seen.

Unfortunately, that's not mission-driven enough for a new clothing brand. If you're considering manufacturing in the

United States (I'll cover more on this in Section 5), realize that factories here pay U.S. prices and use U.S. employees. We can't compete with fast fashion prices and overseas manufacturing.

This is why step one is to figure out your mission and decide what kind of niche market you want to target. And this is where those "limitations" become really valuable to you. You have to figure out a product that means something to someone—and once you do, you've got loyal customers for life.

I've hesitated from mentioning this in the book because I hate discouraging people who want to get involved in fashion. I understand that desire, and I think it's a good one. At the same time, I need to be realistic about the process and the industry, because my whole goal is to help you succeed with your products. To be honest, I do think there's a place for everyone who wants to get involved in the fashion industry in this book— maybe you're overseas and you *can* compete. I think the lessons in this book are still valuable as you're working to design your products and find your angle.

But the bottom line is that anything you dream up can work as long as you can find some unique approach, some niche market that's just waiting to buy your clothes. If your clothes have a function and a purpose—and yes, if they're pretty, adorable, and cute—then you have an avenue to find customers who will absolutely love them. There are plenty of examples in the industry: companies that donate shoes to those in need for every pair bought, companies that have innovated so drastically that their fashionable skirts finally have useful pockets, and so on.

You don't need to solve some kind of humanitarian crisis with your mission. Your products can just satisfy a need that you've identified with a niche market. But that's a crucial step in planning your new clothing brand, and it starts with getting familiar with the niches that are already out there and the types of customers looking to buy your clothing.

Becoming familiar with today's economy of many niches means embracing the notion that you can't serve everyone. In fact, you probably don't want to, because that would mean losing some of the mission and goals that drive you to create—muddying your "why" and reducing the impact of your creativity. You need to create clothing for a specific audience, for a specific reason. More prudently, having a clear purpose attracts customers and increases your bottom line. Not only that, but it also helps you make key decisions during development. As an apparel designer, you'll make countless choices, from fabric to production quantity. Whenever you feel unsure or overwhelmed, you should always come back to your "why."

NAME YOUR COMPANY

If this is your first apparel line, you may be wondering, *Do I need to have a name for my company, even before I start?* In short, the answer is yes. Vendors and factories will take you more seriously when they know they're working with a business. Also, having a name helps you clarify your purpose and see your project as a real venture that takes priority in your life. When coming up with a name, think about something meaningful, unique, and easy to remember.

Here, I recommend striking a balance. Come up with a thoughtful name now, but don't get so hung up on the right one that you get distracted from what really matters, which is what you're doing and why. It's okay if you don't start out with the perfect name. In fact, chances are good you'll change it down the line. It's common for new brands to evolve in their early years, and the right name often comes *after* an audience gets to know a new product. But starting out with a name that's meaningful to you will help imbue the rest of your important decisions with that same focused meaning.

Emma's Story

Meet Emma Almeroth. Throughout this book, we'll share her story as an example of what's possible for new clothing brands like you. Her company, MAI Movement, provides yoga studio owners with well-crafted apparel that's fully customizable with their branding. Inspired by the belief that success requires overcoming judgment and self-doubt, she's built a business that reflects her values.

Emma's company began when she was in design school at the University of Wisconsin Stout. She and two friends launched seasonal collections with small quantities of each style. One had been practicing yoga and mentioned how much the mantra "I am enough" landed for her in class. "We all gasped and looked at each other," Emma now explains. "As twenty-three-year-olds, we were struggling to find our path, feeling like we should have way more figured out. That mantra hit us deep in our core."

And so, her company's name was born: I Am Enough. "That was our mantra, so I put it into my name. We went with it!" she says. But, as with most new brands, things evolved over time. Two or three years in, Emma had a clearer vision of her customer and products. She wanted to describe better what her apparel was, while honoring her original mission.

Soon MAI Movement came to be—a creative take on *I AM,* read backwards. (MAI is pronounced the same as *my.*) "I think it's important to have a place you're starting with," she points out now. "So it's okay to start with what

> you think is going to be your name, and if it changes, it
> changes." Emma's experience in naming her company is
> a key example of why a thoughtful name is so important
> at the beginning, even if it changes later on—that initial
> name gave her purpose and focus. It helped her find her
> "why." And it informed her subsequent decisions, allow-
> ing her to continue to grow and develop her company
> and her vision.

DEFINE YOUR MISSION

Especially for new brands that serve a narrow market, it's critical to know why you exist. Before jumping into the process
of designing and manufacturing, take a step back. Get clear
on why your clothing needs to live in the world. Figure out
what needs your products satisfy, what markets they serve,
and what customers they delight and inspire. As you build and
run your business, you'll come back to your mission, time and
time again.

Having a strong mission attracts buyers, motivates workers (including you), and helps you make decisions along the
way. And let's be clear: You are about to make *a lot* of decisions. Building an apparel line involves high-level choices such
as who you'll work with and a stream of tiny decisions like,
"Exactly which shade of copper should that snap be?"

Because your mission guides everything you do, it needs
to be easy to understand. Keep it short, and avoid getting so
creative that people don't know what they're getting. At The
Apparel Mentor, our mission is "Relentlessly helping new
apparel entrepreneurs succeed by mentoring through the process of idea to manufacturing." In one sentence, we tell *what*

we do, *how* we do it, and *who* we do it for. Our mission governs our design and business choices—*and* it lets the people we work with understand what to expect from us.

WRITE YOUR MISSION STATEMENT

You should be able describe your mission in one to two sentences. When writing your statement, cover what you do, how you do it, and who you do it for. Don't worry if this takes time. I expect you to experiment. Write one version, then run it by several people—ideally those in your target market. Do they understand what you mean? What questions do they have? Did they interpret something differently than you intended? Sift through these things and try again.

Rewrite the statement as needed, until it feels right. This statement can be a great way to introduce your brand. Use it as your elevator pitch, and you'll find out quickly whether it resonates with others, or even makes sense! Especially if you're new to running a business, you may be surprised at how challenging it can be to get your mission statement right.

When you live and breathe your idea, it makes perfect sense in your own head. But when others learn about it for the first time, they may see something different than what you meant. If this happens, don't get discouraged. Innocent misunderstandings of a new brand are common at first. Take it as a sign that you need to use simpler wording or get to the point in a new way. Remember, even if *you* think your mission is perfect, the only thing that matters is for your *customers* to understand it, because their opinions are the ones that will determine your eventual success. Try again; you'll nail it soon enough.

And even once you're happy, you'll still want to check back over time to make sure your mission statement matches your brand. In fact, we recommend you revisit it on an annual basis—no matter how established your brand becomes.

One litmus test I have of whether a mission statement is strong enough is if someone tells me theirs and then proceeds to explain what it is they mean. If you find yourself explaining what you do after you say your mission statement, I would say try again until no additional explanation is needed.

SET YOUR CORE VALUES

Whether they realize it or not, every company operates according to core values. These values guide interactions at every level, from big decisions to daily interactions. And even if these values aren't said out loud, they can be *felt* by everyone who encounters the company. Think of a time you had a bad experience with a product or service.

Maybe you went into a restaurant hoping for a certain food you crave, then realized they value fresh seasonal ingredients over providing a variety of options. Or perhaps you bought a plane ticket on a budget airline, only to discover that not being able to book an assigned seat stressed you out too much to make it worth it. In both cases, there was nothing inherently right or wrong about what was provided. The problem was a mismatch in values. In the same way, your clothing line should be made for the people whose core values match yours.

At The Apparel Mentor, our core values are as follows:

- We are driven to succeed.
- We embrace change and are eager to learn.

- Personal and professional growth are equally important.
- We value team collaboration and trust each other.
- We are solution-oriented, independent thinkers.
- As we do the above, we stay calm, cool, and collected.

Every year, I revisit this list with my staff. We decide if anything has changed since we last reviewed the list. Most of the time, no major changes are needed. But it's also not uncommon for us to make tweaks, based on how we've grown or changed.

When you're ready, write your own core values. This list should contain about five values, and should not exceed seven. As with the mission statement, keep them brief and easy to understand.

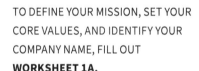

TO DEFINE YOUR MISSION, SET YOUR
CORE VALUES, AND IDENTIFY YOUR
COMPANY NAME, FILL OUT
WORKSHEET 1A.

IDENTIFY AN INSPIRATION BRAND

Several times throughout this book, I'll ask you to refer to an inspiration brand. Simply put, this is a brand in your space that inspires you. Maybe you're a golfer who has a pant that's your go-to because it's slim but breathable. Maybe you've been loyal to a swimwear line because it's the only one that *gets* your body type. Or maybe you've always been partial to a certain fleece collection, just because you like the vibe of their store.

During this lesson, you'll identify an inspiration brand. It should be something in your space that serves a clientele that's similar to yours. At key times during your development process, this brand will provide a benchmark for you. It will be a guide as you articulate what features or services your line should have. It'll help you make decisions, when in doubt. And perhaps most important, it'll serve as a communication tool, when telling your vendors what you mean.

The question you'll need to ask yourself, over and over, is "Why would somebody buy from *me*?" What makes your product unique? Imagine your product hanging on a rack next to your competitors. Why will customers want your product versus the next one? Sometimes, the answer will be about the product. Other times, the differentiator will have more to do with the service you provide.

Emma's Story

When Emma started her yoga line, she was an instructor and loyal user of Lululemon apparel. She felt comfortable and cozy in their clothes, which featured technical details that looked cool. Her yogi friends also enjoyed Lululemon's style. One of these people was Lindsey, who owned a boutique studio where Emma was an instructor. As it happens, Lindsey was about to become Emma's first customer.

When Emma began dreaming about stocking Lindsey's store with apparel, Lululemon became a great inspiration brand for discussion. Their tanks and leggings provided movement that both women liked, but Lindsey wanted something Lululemon couldn't provide: The ability to customize pieces with her studio's brand. Seeing this gap in the marketplace, Emma saw opportunity. This realization led to a strategy that would define her future: She would differentiate herself by providing custom printing.

Another differentiator was the fact that she'd chosen studios, not individuals, as her customer. This path gave Emma clear direction as she developed her first designs. Lindsey values quality in her studio, which caters to clients who want a bespoke experience. To meet this need, Emma focused on high-quality fabric with exceptional fit. She made sure necklines, waists, and other key body parts felt just right: gaping, sliding, and chafing simply wouldn't do.

This required troubleshooting patterns, often multiple times. She didn't quit until her high standards were met. For this reason, Emma narrowed her line to a few key styles. Prioritizing quality over quantity, Emma started with a small line. Over time, her customer base would grow. But until then, she committed to keeping her product line manageable.

Emma's use of Lululemon as an inspiration brand allowed her to make decisions that matched her mission and goals, providing her with a benchmark at key decision points. Importantly, she helped refine her vision of her products by emulating what she liked about Lululemon products *and* by diverging and innovating when she found that her individual ideas were better for her target market. Ultimately, having an inspiration brand enabled her to achieve her overall goals more efficiently and with greater clarity.

TO IDENTIFY YOUR INSPIRATION BRAND
AND WHAT MAKES YOU UNIQUE,
FILL OUT **WORKSHEET 1B.**

LESSON 2

IDENTIFY YOUR TARGET MARKET

Lesson Objectives

In this lesson, you will:

- ▶ Create a profile of your ideal client that includes a variety of factors like demographics, values, and lifestyle.
- ▶ Consider the economy of scale. Like it or not, the client's income is very important.
- ▶ Revisit your inspiration brand through the lens of your target client.

Once you're clear on your mission and values, you must define something equally important: *Who are your people?* After all, everything you make is for them. They're the reason your brand can sustain itself. Without them, any piece of clothing you may dream up is meaningless. A common pitfall for new apparel designers is that they get so excited about their product—colors, trims, shapes—that they forget to slow down and fall in love with their target market.

Yes, you heard me right. It's my belief that new clothing brands shouldn't just *like* their people, they should shower them with *love*. Find out their hopes and fears. Know their hangouts. Pay attention to their favorite colors. Even if you think you already know your people, do not skip this lesson. Not only is it fun, but it also makes everything easier. From design to marketing, the process is more successful when owners know their ideal client.

CREATE A PROFILE OF YOUR IDEAL CLIENT

I know you're excited to get into the designing portion, but *it's really important not to skip this step*. Getting clear on your ideal client now, will save you considerable time, money, and headaches later. This involves considering a variety of factors that define your market. The more specific you can be, the better. If you're a new business owner, narrowing your niche may feel counterintuitive. Many new designers fear that a narrow market will mean narrow sales. In fact, the opposite is true.

For new clothing brands, success comes from serving a specific market exceptionally well. The more you know about the people you're serving, the better you'll connect with them. Think of it as picking your muse. If you can picture a specific person to design for, they can serve as your source of inspiration for every decision you make. From choosing fabric to creating social media, you must speak directly to your beloved people. When customers feel heard, they have a positive experience with your brand. And when they feel good, they come back for more. Not only that, but they're likely to recommend you to their friends, who are likely to share similar qualities.

TO CREATE A PROFILE OF YOUR IDEAL
CLIENT, FILL OUT **WORKSHEET 2A.**

LOOK AT STRATEGIC CONSIDERATIONS

ECONOMY OF SCALE

Economy of scale is an important concept in the apparel industry. When it comes to producing many copies of an item—such as a book, car, or pair of jeans—manufacturing costs go down the more items you produce. This affects the entire life cycle of the product too, not just the quantity of stock you want to develop. For example, the preproduction process is intensive. It involves getting the item's components to the factory and ready to go. It takes a lot of hard work, even if you're just producing *one* item. But once the factory is in motion, then making more of the item is simply a matter of repetition.

Now is not the time to get in the weeds about details like quantity and pricing. That said, you must ensure your apparel idea makes financial sense. Some designers serve high-end consumers, others reach a mass market, and endless possibilities exist between. No approach is inherently right or wrong, but you should do a gut check: Is your overall plan realistic?

For example, there's nothing wrong with serving an audience at a lower income level. But you need to consider the economy of scale. In order to make a profit, you may need to sell tens of thousands of units. Especially in your early days, this may not be a viable option. If your resources are limited, you should pay careful attention to your target market. Simply put, they must be able to afford your products at the level you're able to produce them.

Consider the activewear company Fabletics. Their mission involves affordability, and they have proven it's possible to carry this out. As a new clothing brand, however, you must keep in mind that they had the capital to make it work. From the beginning, they had strong marketing behind them and considerable funds to invest. They were able to produce high enough quantities of their products to offset the lower prices and reach their markets. That's not something everyone will be able to do, and as a new clothing brand, you should consider the balance between capital and pricing before you invest your time and effort into something that won't work out in the long term.

Emma's Story

"My favorite way to pick a client is to get really, really specific," Emma says. "Whether it be someone you hang out with or someone you see around town, think of an actual person. My person is my studio owner, Lindsey. I know her." Any time Emma needs to make a decision about her product, she thinks of Lindsey and others like her. "She's in her forties, she's graduated from university. She's passionate and playful, and she adores her French bulldog. Her annual household income is over $100,000. She likes saving for things like trips and taking her family places."

All these details give Emma a clear vision of how to serve studio owners like Lindsey. For example, when she creates a marketing campaign, she factors in things like age, income, and travel. She designs her marketing to suit what will appeal to Lindsey, knowing that there are many other potential clients just like her who will be drawn to the same sorts of imagery. Her Instagram feed includes aspirational photos of yogis in hip, gorgeous studios. Their tanks and leggings display custom studio designs, while models demonstrate impressive moves.

Lindsey's biggest life goal is to continue growing her number of studios. She has two now, and she's constantly looking to expand. She doesn't have a lot of time to order apparel, so Emma's approach must be efficient. "When I come in, I need to be on point." Emma explains. "I'll say, 'Here are the products I recommend for next season.' I show fabrics to suit her style, and I come prepared with custom designs she can print on the clothes."

"I make it easy for her," Emma elaborates. "I give tidbits on how to provide apparel for different locations. Her clients look for trends in the cities she visits, like Portland and New York. She's always on the move."

From sales conversations to design decisions, Emma's brand supports her studio owners, who've turned out to be a desirable match for Emma's economy of scale. Matching her business plans to what her ideal client is looking for has enabled Emma to achieve a satisfactory economy of scale and make her new clothing brand work for her clients.

Looking back, she's grateful she didn't build her business around the grad students she originally wanted to serve. Though her original plan may have been personally fulfilling, the numbers didn't add up. Back in Emma's days at design school, she and her friends had internships that paid minimum wage, if that. As much as she wanted to make clothing for students, Emma didn't have the capital to support the design and manufacturing process that providing low-cost, affordable pieces would have required. Identifying the right client for her resources and goals took time. But in the end, her dedication proved more than worthwhile.

REVISIT YOUR INSPIRATION BRAND

Throughout this book, there are several key points where you'll refer to an inspiration brand as a point of reference for decision making. Now that you've gained more clarity around your target customer, revisit the inspiration brand you identified in Lesson 1. Maybe having a muse will confirm your original choice. Or maybe you'll see things differently now, and select a different inspiration brand. Whichever choice you make, remember that these inspirations and missions are always fluid; they're designed to help *you* figure out the best approach to your business, not to lock you into a set way of thinking about your brand.

WHAT YEARLY INCOME DOES YOUR IDEAL CUSTOMER HAVE? WHAT PRICE POINT DO YOU WANT YOUR GARMENT TO HAVE? DO THESE TWO ITEMS MAKE SENSE TOGETHER? IN OTHER WORDS, CAN YOUR IDEAL CLIENT AFFORD THIS PRICE POINT? TO REVIEW THESE STRATEGIC CONSIDERATIONS, FILL OUT **WORKSHEET 2B.**

LESSON 3

SKETCH YOUR DESIGN

Lesson Objectives

In this lesson, you will:

► Think through details of the garment you envision, including fit and features. Use existing clothing as your inspiration.

► Draw a simple sketch, both front and back.

► Do this for every product you want to make, with five as your max.

Once you've defined your mission and ideal client, you can start to focus on design. Ultimately, designing a garment is a process that involves multiple vendors, including a specialist who makes technical sketches. But let's put first things first. For this lesson, all you need to do is get your idea out of your head and onto paper.

Doing this requires no special skills. You don't even have to be good at drawing! This isn't about being pretty. Instead, the goal is to think through your idea and then tell others about it. Keep it simple.

THINK THROUGH THE DETAILS

If you've ever binge-watched a fashion-design competition, you may think design sketches need be works of art. After all, the designers on shows like Project Runway make it look easy to draw stunning sketches. But if there's one thing I want you to know about this step, it's this: Your sketch does not need to be pretty!

In fact, when it comes to your early design sketches, aesthetics aren't the goal. Instead, the point is to get your idea out of your head and onto paper. Over the years I've designed hundreds of lines of clothes, and I am not a good artist. (If you saw my sketches, you might agree.) Instead, as a factory owner who helps new clothing brands bring their own designs to life, I'll tell you what *does* matter for your sketch: getting clear about the features you want and capturing them in a form you can show others. The prettiest, most aesthetic design sketches won't be worth anything to your new clothing brand if they don't clearly demonstrate the features you're looking for and provide guidance and appeal to others, including potential clients.

Especially if you're new to apparel design, you may not be used to noticing how many details go into clothing. For example, necklines are really important. They can come in a surprising variety of shapes, like boat neck, asymmetrical, halter, and sweetheart, just to name a few. And how the neckline fits makes all the difference. Think about it this way: Do you want cleavage to show or not? That's a pretty important question to answer when you're selecting what you want to wear, and answering this single question alone involves a variety of design decisions that greatly impact how your buyer will feel when wearing your apparel.

Lest you think that all my efforts with clients have turned into major successes, I want to share an example of a colossal failure and what I learned from it. Sometimes I simply can't figure out how to help someone who wants to work with us because they haven't taken the necessary time to think through all the details—and sometimes that results in some pretty serious consequences down the line.

One of the biggest pitfalls in this line of work is doing things out of order. There's a reason I've ordered these lessons the way I have. There's a reason I insist that you follow them in order. I communicated with a potential client once who wanted our help in launching their product. These were well-intentioned people who simply didn't understand the industry, and they did things all out of order. They came to us and essentially said, "Listen, we've already bought something like 10,000 yards of this fabric because we're trying to hit this deadline we set for our launch. But we just can't get the product to fit. We've tried and tried, and we can't make it work. Can you help us?"

And, you know, my heart ached for them—but the answer was simply that *No, I couldn't help them.* You see, they'd jumped to Lesson 19 of this book and skipped over the rest of the process. We evaluated their fabric, and I had to tell them that the 10,000 yards of fabric they'd purchased simply wouldn't work at all for the product they had in mind. It was the wrong fabric. It just wouldn't do what they wanted it to do. There really wasn't any way I could help at that point. And that kind of story just breaks my heart, but it's the unfortunate reality of the industry.

I should also mention that thinking through the details is also very important when considering the purpose and intention of the product. I know I've covered this already, but it's important, so I'm hitting it again. Sometimes people have an idea for an item of clothing but they don't have any real reason for wanting to make it happen. They don't know why they're making it or why people would want it. I ask them: "Why would somebody buy your product when it's hanging next to another one by a major brand?" If you're going to make a polo, and you're trying to sell it next to a rack of Nike polos, why would people pick yours? Nike already has plenty of fine polos; what sets yours apart?

It's surprising how often people don't have a good answer to these kinds of questions. But the fact is, Nike makes polos. They have that process down. Everyone golfs in a Nike polo. How are you going to make people buy yours instead? *Why* should they buy yours instead? If you *do* have a good answer— perfect! You've thought through the details! Let's go make it happen! But if you can't answer that simple question of *why*, then that means it's time for you to take a hard look at your plans and figure out what the next step is.

Now, I don't want you to be overly worried at this point. There's plenty of time to figure things out, tweak your sketches, and make adjustments. But I want to impress upon you the importance of thinking through the details first before you invest significant time and resources into something that might not end up how you envisioned.

START WITH AN INSPIRATION PIECE

To kick off your sketching process, start by gathering inspiration from existing clothes. If you're making a winter hoodie, gather five favorites from your closet. Look online for hoodies you love. Examine each closely, noting what you like and what you don't. Are there any trims, like zipper pulls or buttons?

Does the sleeve have a thumb hole? What kind of finishing is used at the hemline?

At this stage, you can't predict exactly which embellishments will ultimately grace your garment. Many factors will dictate that, particularly the resources you can devote. During the sourcing process (Section 2), you'll discover what's actually possible. For now, let's capture the features that matter most. Maybe you have a ton of ideas. That's okay, for the time being. You'll have plenty of chances to narrow things down. Think of your ideal client. Ask yourself, What features would *they* want? Make sure any features you add are in alignment with your mission.

Emma's Story

When Emma founded her yoga-apparel company, she launched just four pieces: a basic tank, a basic legging, a fashion tank, and a bra. For each, she began by gathering clothes she already had or liked, then studied their features. She analyzed what she liked and didn't about each inspiration piece, and the process helped her envision her own line.

"Starting with an inspiration product is a really, really good idea," she says. "When I started designing my tank top, I looked at other tank tops I had. Do I want a scoop neck or V neck? Do I want a high neckline? Then I worked on the back. Do I want spaghetti straps or a racer back?" At first, designing a tank top may have seemed simple. But as Emma's process demonstrated, there are many decisions that go into every piece. And each decision had an effect on the overall outcome of the piece, so she had to be thoughtful about her choices and really consider what she wanted with her brand.

As Emma's business evolved, she gained access to an additional resource: her patternmaker. "There are things your patternmaker can help you with," she says, "like things that are borderline technical." Even so, she's quick to point out that your original hand sketch is not about being perfect. Instead, start where you can. Get your idea out of your head and onto paper. You can make all the tweaks you need to when you've actually got something solid to work with.

DRAW A SIMPLE SKETCH

Once you have a sense for the features you want, it's time to make your sketch. You'll draw two versions, one from the front and one from the back. Draw as if the garment is lying flat on a table, or hanging from a hanger. Accompany your drawing with a callout to each feature, so viewers won't miss a detail you want them to see. In addition, find or take a photo of an inspiration garment. Together, your sketch and the photo will be your tool for communicating with upcoming vendors, like your patternmaker. (If you already have a patternmaker, ask their opinion as you sketch.)

Use any drawing implement you like: pen, pencil, marker. It doesn't have to be fancy. In fact, simple shapes like circles and arrows are particularly valuable! If you're picturing a special kind of pocket, draw it. When you say *hip-hugger short,* what exactly do you mean? If that capri you've been dreaming of is high-waisted, depict the proportion.

Remember, your product does not yet exist. The only place it lives is in your mind. That is, until you take a few minutes to make your hand sketches. If you know your industry well, this step may be easy for you. But if apparel is new to you or you're intimidated, reach out to someone who can guide you, as you sketch your ideas. Or please check out if becoming a member in the Apparel Mentor community would be a good fit for you.

— — Mentor Moment — —

An Example: Maternity Swim Coverup

Let's use one of my clients as an example. After identifying a gap in the marketplace, she wanted to make a maternity swim coverup. In our early design conversations, she ended up making two versions of her sketch. The first one provided me with a good sense of the shape, but I had to ask her lots of questions about the details. By the second round, she'd developed a sketch that was still very simple to look at (which, again, is *totally fine*), but called out important features.

This time, her sketch was surrounded by words like "high waist," "zipper," and "hood," each with an arrow pointing to its corresponding feature. In all, the designer wanted a high waist, a ring for sunglasses, a zipper, a hood, a long sleeve, light cotton fabric, and a maxi length. Along with the sketch, she provided a photo of a model wearing a swim coverup from the inspiration brand she'd identified. Between the sketch and the photo, I now had enough information to see what trims and embellishments the designer really wanted.

You can see how simple and straightforward her sketch is. It's certainly not a fine piece of art. And that's great! Because it includes all of the relevant details about her piece, and it displays them clearly to the people who need that information. This is what you're aiming for when you're creating your own design sketches for your planned products.

REPEAT FOR EACH OF YOUR PIECES

After finishing your first sketch, repeat this step for each item you want to produce. Depending on your goals, you must choose how many pieces to launch. For first-time designers, I recommend anywhere between one and five items. This decision involves many factors, which you'll encounter as you progress through design. Just because you sketch something now, doesn't mean you're obligated to make it, or that your plan won't change. In fact, you can expect your plan to evolve as you go.

Even so, it's important to level-set your expectations now, early in the process. Especially if you're a new designer, it's critical to avoid biting off more than you can chew. If you have an abundance of ideas, choose your top five and sketch those. (If the thought of narrowing feels hard for you, think of it this way: Forcing yourself to choose is a valuable exercise in expressing your mission.)

When you're ready, get sketching. And have fun!

DESCRIBE YOUR GARMENT(S) HERE. USE DESCRIPTORS LIKE WHAT TYPE NECKLINE, SLEEVES, LENGTH, POCKETS ETC.... EVEN IF YOU ARE NOT AN ARTIST GETTING DESCRIPTIVE WORDS ON PAPER IS A GOOD START! TO THINK THROUGH DETAILS AND SKETCH YOUR DESIGN, COMPLETE **WORKSHEET 3.**

LESSON 4

DECIDE YOUR APPROACH: DIY OR FULL PARTNER?

Lesson Objectives

In this lesson, you will:

- ▶ Explore the steps required to build an apparel line.
- ▶ Weigh two approaches new designers can take: DIY or Full Partner.
- ▶ Decide which approach is the best fit for you.

Launching a line is a rewarding way to find purpose, serve an audience, and build a profitable business. But if you're not prepared, the process can lead to frustration, financial strain, or both. Let's set realistic expectations from the start. As with any small business, making an apparel line requires time, money, and energy. You as the founder must decide how those resources get used.

Are you a scrappy startup with plans to do much of this yourself? Or do you have the resources to start with a larger team of support? There's no right or wrong answer, unless you neglect to be intentional. Here, you'll consider two approaches you might take: DIY or Full Partner.

As with any small business, making an apparel line requires time, money, and energy. But I've created countless products for my own brands and for clients. I've developed a process specifically geared toward new designers like you. Our mission at The Apparel Mentor is to help you learn the ropes of this industry, which is weighted heavily in favor of big brands. As a new designer, you're bound to face barriers along the way, but our tools help you navigate around them.

After guiding hundreds of new designers, we've narrowed the style development process down into ten major steps. In this lesson, we'll give you an overview. Then you'll decide which approach suits you best for taking this on.

WHY THE BIG PICTURE MATTERS

Have you ever made a recipe without reading the instructions first? Maybe you got halfway through before realizing a key ingredient was missing. When that happened, maybe you found a neighbor who had what you needed, maybe you "made do" with a substitution, or maybe your creation got ruined. Either way, your process got interrupted. Things took longer than they needed to, and your food's quality got compromised. If you'd planned ahead, you'd probably have done things differently.

Consider this lesson your chance to "read the recipe" before stating your apparel line. I'll walk you through a quick overview of every step, from start to finish. Then, I'll offer two approaches for undertaking your project. You'll choose the option that's best for you, and your decision will help you approach the project strategically. You'll begin with a more realistic plan than if you'd simply jumped in, unaware. All of this preliminary decision making and preparation will only serve to clarify your process and remove unnecessary hurdles in making your plans a reality.

Note that this is *not* the time to get caught in the details. Instead, take in the process at a high level. As you do, consider your readiness to tackle the process as a whole. Think about your resources of time, money, and energy. Begin assessing how much of each you have available now, and in the long term. Depending on what you can devote, a DIY approach may be the best fit for you. Or, you may opt to hire a full management partner. Either way is equally valid. The important thing is to choose what's right for you.

THE STEPS OF LAUNCHING AN APPAREL LINE

Okay, now that the context is out of the way, let's dive in! Here are the steps required to make an apparel line, which will help you gauge which path is right for you.

STEP 1: DESIGN

As you communicate with vendors, you must have a reliable way to show them your garment. The more specific you can be, the more efficient and cost effective the process will be, at every step. To achieve this, you'll hire a technical designer to make a detailed, computer-rendered technical sketch of your apparel. This requires finding someone who specializes in your fabric type and draws the visuals in a way that factories can read.

STEP 2: SOURCE YOUR FABRIC AND TRIMS

As with all the steps, this one involves a surprising number of micro-steps. Ultimately, you'll place an order for the fabric and trims needed for your garments. For this, you'll adopt a non-retail mindset; learn fabric basics; find an existing garment with the fabric you'll want; determine specifications for your materials; learn the tiers of fabric vendors; discover ways to approach suitable vendors; and source materials that are reliable, affordable, and stylish.

STEP 3: MAKE YOUR FIRST PATTERN

Here, you'll hire a patternmaker to develop your first pattern. This is a specialized skill that is both an art and a science. Patternmakers have an excellent understanding of sewing, are detail oriented, and know computer design software. Expect to answer many questions about features you may or may not have considered before. In some cases, they'll provide multiple versions for your consideration. Other times, your vision will be so clear that you'll need only one pattern from the get-go.

STEP 4: MAKE YOUR FIRST PROTOTYPE (A.K.A., SAMPLE)

Now that you have your technical sketch, you're ready to make your first prototype! The point of prototypes is to identify any problems in the design. Creating them is an iterative process that can take anywhere from one to three months. Many new designers underestimate what it takes to get prototypes right, and they fail to see how important this is, until it's too late. But developing a thorough prototype saves you considerable time and money, because you'll eliminate any flaws before producing multiple copies.

You'll identify a sample sewer, who will take the design and turn it into a garment. As they sew, they'll note anything that doesn't work according to plan. They'll provide you with an actual garment, ready to be tried on by fit models who represent your target market.

— — Mentor Moment — —

A Note about Terms

In the apparel industry, you'll hear the word "sample" for what I call a *prototype*. Though these terms refer to the same thing, I use *prototype* intentionally. Over the years, I've watched too many aspiring designers make the mistake of breezing past making samples. They heard the word "sample" and envision something cheap, disposable, or simplistic—something that won't have any bearing on their ultimate product. Often, the result is disastrous, costing the designer precious money, time, and energy.

I much prefer the word *prototype*, and here's a little background why.

I've mentioned before that I spent some time working with big design companies and factories. Even while I was freelancing during this period, I was often involved in visiting the factories themselves to inspect materials and products and meet more closely with vendors and other involved parties. For a while, I was traveling overseas pretty often, working on starting up a women's wear company and getting involved in other projects. Between 2004 and 2010, I spent a *lot* of time traveling to factories in South America, Central America, and Asia.

In my experiences there, I saw the often poor working conditions and meager wages for factory workers. Those trips informed my ongoing mission to help focus fashion manufacturing in the United States and to improve the quality of working conditions throughout the industry. But the point of this story right now is something else I observed during my visits to these overseas factories.

When I was working in this role, I wasn't some bigwig that went into the office to manage workers—I was a designer, a developer, and I wanted to get things *done*. If things weren't happening, if the work wasn't coming along the way we wanted it to, I got involved and got things figured out. If we had a problem, I stepped in to meet with the right people and fix it.

One of my freelance customers was a stroller company. We were focused on designing some of the fabric parts of the stroller they were planning to produce. The factory they were using just wasn't getting it right. There was a lot of back and forth, but ultimately I realized I just had to meet with the workers in person and get everyone on the same page. So I flew out to their factory and met with the pattern makers and the sewers and everyone else involved. I wasn't there on some fancy tour; I saw the underbelly, the workrooms, the sewing stations. I worked *with* those people.

I've already talked about how clarity in communications is paramount, so I won't belabor that point again—though it was *very* useful to be in the same room as my collaborators and show them *exactly* what I wanted done. But the other really useful lesson was in using the right terminology to honor the work that was being done.

I'm not just referring to language barriers, though that was a big part of it. What I mean is that most people don't quite understand everything that goes into designing clothes. Even plenty of people who work in the industry have what amounts to a dismissive view of the whole process. They talk about making apparel samples. They hire pattern makers. They give these cutesy little homemaker names to all of the aspects of the industry. I understand where that comes from, of course. But I also understand the way it makes people thing about the work being done. This kind of terminology makes apparel design sound like a hobby, a pastime, a fun little fling that we engage in on the weekends to keep us busy.

But the work that I'm talking about in this book is much, much more than that. The work that you're putting into your mission and brand and designs is so much more than that. Designing clothes is *engineering* at its heart, and it's just as difficult as the work done in all of the other traditionally male industries—no different than designing a chair or a computer mouse or whatever else. The talent and skill and dedication required are just as intense as in any of those other industries. Designing apparel is amazingly complicated, and the language we use should reflect that.

One thing I'm still so proud of is my decision to deliberately change the language I use for certain aspects of our work. We make *prototypes*. We hire *pattern engineers*. We use terms that confer the proper respect to the work being done. In doing so, we recognize the effort required in designing clothes and the sacrifices involved. These terms have become a lot more common nationwide, and that's another major reward of the work I've been a part of. Using the right words—like the word *prototype*—can have a huge impact on the quality of the work throughout the whole process.

I've found that using the word *prototype* helps people understand the importance of creating test runs. Just as a car manufacturer relies on prototypes to identify design flaws to ensure safety and performance, you are responsible for developing a reliable product too. The sooner you embrace the idea that you're building a product, the more ready you'll be for the dedication required to get it right. Your prototypes don't have to be perfect—in fact, they certainly won't be!—but they should be the product of care and attention to avoid costly mistakes down the road.

STEP 5: EVALUATE THE SAMPLE

Before manufacturing any garment, you must ensure it's free of flaws. Flaws can come in many forms, like puckering, open seams, or mismeasuring. Such defects can be caused by the pattern, fabric, or both. You may or may not be qualified to conduct the evaluation yourself. If you don't have a strong sewing background, it will be nearly impossible for you to anticipate the types of issues a sample could reveal. Even if you're following the DIY approach, you may have to hire someone for this step.

STEP 6: COMPILE A LIST OF REVISIONS

Expect to make changes to your first sample. This is a necessary part of the process. During your evaluation, you may encounter suggestions for revisions from several people—your sample sewer, the professional you hired to evaluate it, and yourself. Make sure you've compiled these into a format that's easy to follow. You'll need to provide clear instructions to your sample sewer.

STEP 7: MAKE YOUR SECOND SAMPLE

Have your sample sewer make a revised version. Make sure it incorporates all the recommendations you'd identified earlier, and that no new issues have been revealed. You may or may not get it right this time around, so be prepared to repeat Steps 5–7 until your garment is ready for production.

STEP 8: GRADE YOUR PATTERN

Up till this point, you've been looping through one size only, called your *base size*. This step is where you'll account for the additional sizes you'll produce. There's no hard-and-fast rule for how many sizes to make, but I've observed a trend for marketability in the apparel industry: offering five sizes. *Grading* a pattern means turning a single pattern into multiple sizes. You'll hire a specialist for this task, called a pattern grader. Their role is more complicated than it may sound.

STEP 9: SEW ALL THE SIZES

Provide your sample sewer with the patterns, and ask them to sew a version of each.

STEP 10: MAKE YOUR FINAL TECH PACK

To produce your garment, a manufacturer needs instructions for all details such as measurements, fabric, trims, and colors. This requires a specialized document called a *tech pack*. (Think of a tech pack as a blueprint for a house.)

Hire a technical designer to make your tech pack, which includes drawings and written directives. This step is a critical culmination of all the work you've done so far. As manager of this significant project, you'll need to ensure that all the details make it into this document.

STEP 11: MANUFACTURE

This phase involves determining the appropriate vendor to manufacture your garment, which is a process, in and of itself. Your relationship with your manufacturer can make or break your success, or—at the very least—influence your willingness to go through it again next time.

Some manufacturers operate as full-service operations, from sourcing materials to packaging your final garment. Others offer partial services or function in a piecemeal manner. Find out which is the best fit for you.

Then, to find the right manufacturer, do your homework. You'll research things like what brands they've worked with, quantities they produce, and timelines they deliver. You'll also want to know about their certifications, contract requirements, approval process, and team.

Once you've found your manufacturer, you'll provide your tech pack, sign a contract, and communicate with them at key points throughout. Completing your garment can take any-where from 6 months to 2 years' time.

After this is done, you've earned yourself a big celebration!

Next up: You'll need to manage a variety of things, such as warehousing, inventory tracking, shipping, and marketing. Though these things are outside the bounds of this book, we want to make sure you're considering them from the begin-ning. Remember, your diligence in planning and preparing for all steps of this process will help you streamline your work and improve your chances of a successful product launch.

EXPLORE TWO APPROACHES

You've just heard what it takes to turn your idea into a finished apparel product. Now, take a step back. Consider the resources available to you and compare them to the overall process as outlined here. Over the next year or two, how much time, money, and energy can you devote to launching your line?

New designers are not all the same. Some are hobby sewists starting a business for the first time. Others are long-time entrepreneurs who are new to making clothing. Others fall into a variety of categories in between. Some aren't ready to start a line just yet, but they're motivated to learn how—to prepare for when they are.

Regardless of where you fall on this spectrum, you'll benefit from weighing two approaches: DIY or Full Partner, both of which are outlined below.

A QUICK NOTE ABOUT VENDORS

Regardless of which approach you choose, creating an apparel line means overseeing a variety of vendors. If you've ever planned a wedding, you know what it's like to communicate with multiple vendors simultaneously about the countless number of details. If you're not already thinking of yourself as project manager, begin doing so from here on out.

There's no way to predict exactly how many vendors your project will need. But as a rule of thumb, be prepared to hire anywhere from 7 to 10 contractors, over the course of your project. (This count does *not* include vendors needed for business operations and marketing.)

Vendors needed to create an apparel line include:

1. Tech designer
2. Trim vendor
3. Fabric vendor
4. Pattern maker
5. Sample sewer
6. Patternmaker/ grader
7. Manufacturer

In some cases, the same individual or company will cover more than one of these roles. Others specialize. No matter what, each vendor will bring to the table their own processes, values, pricing, timing, commitment, and level of expertise. The key message here is this: Get ready to take charge, communicate, and get organized!

APPROACH #1: DIY

This approach is best for designers whose budget is limited. Hello, scrappy startup types! Under the DIY model, you'll become a project manager extraordinaire. You'll take ownership over every stage. You'll become a master of overall strategy and minute details. Your timeline will extend, you'll communicate like the dickens, and keeping things on track will be up to you. Under this approach, you must get used to the idea that you'll spend the next two years or so navigating an industry that's not set up for new clothing brands like you.

In addition to making countless decisions about garments, you'll be called to explore a network of vendors who seem to operate underground. Patternmakers, sewers, factories, and other specialists are used to serving big companies. They use industry jargon that can seem disorienting. They may or may not list their services online. If your native language is English, their primary tongue may differ from yours. Most industry professionals aren't set up to show you the ropes. You need them more than they need you, and more often than not, they know it.

So, yes, the DIY approach requires plenty of grit! But for those who embrace the role, the process can be incredibly rewarding, financially profitable, and fun. Your apparel line can turn you into your own boss and help you serve people whose needs you truly care about. I truly believe new clothing brands are the future of this industry, and I'm committed to helping people like you become the agents of this important change.

And hey—a word of encouragement. Too often we have a picture of a scrappy DIYer who's constantly a little frazzled and a little overworked, pouring in hours of late night and early morning labor on a passion project, just to make a piece or two—something to be proud of and to make all the extremely hard work seem worth it. And yeah, that can be pretty accurate. It *is* hard work, no matter what route you take. But there's also a lot of satisfaction down that road—and success, too, if you keep at it.

I started out during my freelancing period. I was making patterns and designs and samples in my living room with my friends. I started realizing that this was the craziest industry I'd ever seen—and that maybe there was a way I could make it a little less crazy, make it accessible to other people looking to get their clothing out into the world and into the hands of the right customers. I started up a website to help other people. I got some attention through word of mouth. I kept working hard—and we just grew and grew and grew *and grew and grew*—and eventually I couldn't keep it all in my house anymore, so we moved into a real building to keep working. After that, we started doing our first real production runs instead of hiring other factories to make our products. We had a little production facility going. And we kept helping other people. For a long time, we were one of maybe two or three resources in the entire United States for people to get help with a clothing idea. That's still crazy to me, to be honest.

So yeah, if you're going the DIY route, it *is* a lot of hard work. But it's not all sacrifice for a pittance, either. Plenty of new clothing brands have found their niche market, reached their ideal customers, and found lots of success in their work. I certainly have, and now I'm able to help guide others to make their DIY road a little less lonely.

— — Mentor Moment — —

If you identify as a DIYer right now, you are not alone. Guiding others like you is one of the most rewarding parts of my career. Aspiring, driven designers are my people, and I built The Apparel Mentor to serve people like you. In this online community, we work through this book together, taking specific looks at individual approaches to understand the best approach to making your DIY plans a reality. We share our wins, give ideas and encouragement, and provide accountability. To learn more, visit **theapparelmentor.com**.

— — — —

APPROACH #2: FULL PARTNER

If project management isn't your jam, the full-partner approach may suit you best. Maybe you have a tight time frame. Maybe you're ready to prioritize what you do best, like designing amazing clothes. Or perhaps the thought of overseeing countless details and granular decisions makes you cringe in every cell of your body. If you have the resources to devote, hiring a cohesive team can save you considerable time and headaches.

In my early days in this industry, I never dreamed I'd enter into manufacturing. If you'd asked me where I was headed in life, I *never* would have said, "I want to run an on-demand clothing factory in Saint Paul, Minnesota, that employs 90% women and is the only factory of its type in the Midwest." Yet that's what happened, organically over time, as I started serving new apparel brands.

Our apparel mentors have worked with new apparel brands to turn their ideas into a saleable reality. From sketch to launch, we've helped hundreds of aspiring designers make their apparel lines. If that type of arrangement sounds best to you—if what you need is a team of specialists who can walk you through patternmaking, prototyping, fabric selection, and manufacturing—you may be ready for the Full-Partner approach, and I encourage you to research companies that offer these services.

There's no such thing as a one-size-fits all approach. We can't predict exact costs without a consultation, as we customize our work to the unique needs of each project. However, as a general guideline of reference, full partner services cost a minimum of $7K to $10K. Depending on what your personality and resources are like, hiring a full partner be the right avenue for you to get your new clothing brand started and your products into the hands of your ideal clients.

DECIDE WHICH IS BEST FOR YOU

When deciding which approach is best for you, neither is inherently right or wrong. You know yourself best. That said, it's absolutely worth your time to assess your resources now, before diving into your apparel line. As with any business venture, you'll invest time, money, and energy into your beloved project.

Another point about working with partners—in whatever capacity—that is often glossed over is that you don't have to completely abandon what you're already passionate about in order to pursue designing a clothing line. Partnering with other people allows you to draw on their strengths *and* your own!

Many entrepreneurial stories involve someone who identifies a problem in the marketplace, a hole to be filled with something purposeful or functional, an oversight in PR that keeps ideal customers from finding the right products. And those entrepreneurs don't just abandon their successful companies and skills and contacts and enroll into design school to figure out how to solve the problem! Please don't suddenly go to design school because you have an apparel idea. Reading this book instead will teach you what you need to know about being a new brand owner.

If you're a nurse and you've figured out a piece of clothing that would help you and your fellow nurses do your jobs better, don't just give up on your dreams of nursing in order to go to design school. Stay working as a nurse! Keep learning about the nursing world; keep figuring out how to make a product that meets your needs and the needs of those you work with. And then just hire people in the apparel industry that you can collaborate with!

One really common trait of very successful clients I've worked with is that they stick with what they're good at and hire others to make up for their weaknesses. In this book, I'm hoping to give you a good enough understanding of the apparel industry and what it takes to make a line of clothing—but I don't want you to think that you need to become an expert on every aspect of design. I'm not trying to teach you how to make your own patterns or match color schemes. I want to give you a high-level understanding of what starting a new clothing brand involves. And then I want to point you toward the pattern engineers and designers and factories and all the other partners you can collaborate with to achieve success.

I've run into tons of people who have an idea and just start buying sewing machines and yards of cloth and design textbooks. Don't do that! (Unless it's a hobby you're passionate about, of course.) It's not necessary, and it's not going to help you be successful. Figure out what you're good at, find people who are good at other things, and work together to make your products.

Now that you've thought about your approach to having a partner, make a decision. Which approach is right for you? The sooner you can make this decision, the more helpful it'll be as you move forward.

Emma's Story

"I am a DIYer, one hundred percent. What I've learned from that is that I *could* spend all my time doing everything. But it's not a good idea. If I spend all my time on manufacturing, I'm not doing sales or focusing on the business. Managing every part of production is a full-time job. So unless you have a team doing some other parts, like writing a blog, production quickly becomes something you no longer have time for.

"If you have the opportunity, and you can produce the units, find a partner. Then you can have more time building the business. Or maybe it's vice versa. Maybe you love production, and you want someone to do the marketing and operations for you. I can definitely relate to the feeling of 'But I want to know how to do all of it.' Consider that you *do* know a lot of it, and you'll continue to learn. But if you find the right partner, then you don't need to be one hand cutting everything.

"Especially for you DIYers, do whatever you can to surround yourself with others who are in the same boat. You can share resources with each other. In fact, I found most of my vendors through people in my network. They came through my asking, 'Who have you worked with?' As for all my sewing partners, I found them on Craig's List."

HOW MUCH TIME PER WEEK DO YOU HAVE TO DEDICATE TO THIS PROJECT? DO YOU ENJOY OR ARE YOU GOOD AT PROJECT MANAGEMENT? THESE QUESTIONS WILL HELP YOU UNDERSTAND IF YOU SHOULD GO DIY OR FULL PARTNER. TO DECIDE YOUR APPROACH, COMPLETE **WORKSHEET 4.**

YOU MAY FIND IT HELPFUL TO SEE A CHART THAT WALKS YOU THROUGH ESTIMATING LAUNCH DATES, **WORKSHEET 11.**

LESSON 5

NARROW YOUR STYLE OFFERING AND GET TECH SKETCHES MADE

Lesson Objectives

In this lesson, you will:

- ▶ Determine how many styles you'll offer.
- ▶ Create a hand sketch of each style.
- ▶ Solicit feedback from your target market.
- ▶ Hire a technical designer to create a tech sketch for each style.

NARROW YOUR STYLES

After deciding whether you'll be your own project manager or hire a team, it's time to narrow your styles. And, yes, I use the word *narrow* intentionally. New designers can get carried away by dreams of all the clothes they want to make without recognizing what it takes to produce them. Don't get me wrong: Dreaming is a positive and even necessary part of the process. It's great fun to imagine all the different kinds of clothing and accessories you might like to produce. Expressing your creativity that way is essential for getting in the right mindset and figuring out what you're most passionate about.

Yet for me, the *real* fun begins when you eliminate styles. This involves getting clear on your brand's "why," then letting go of any ideas that don't support it. For example, if you're making a maternity yoga line, there's no need for headbands. Sure, they may be fun. But they don't serve the specific needs of pregnant women. You can't wear everything all at once, and you can't make every product you might like all at the same time. It's far better to narrow down and focus on making a smaller number of products the best they can be.

Each item you make adds time, money, and energy to your overall business requirements. For your first line, I strongly recommend limiting yourself to five styles or fewer. You can always add more pieces down the road once you're more established and have a better pipeline for your products. Once you narrow your styles, you'll need to hire a specialist to draw tech sketches that feature design details. These sketches are critical for communicating with vendors like your patternmaker. Do yourself a favor: Don't skip this step!

— — **Mentor Moment** — —

What Counts as a Style?

When I say *style,* I'm referring to shapes, *not* colors or sizes. Let's say you want to launch a streetwear line. Five styles might mean a skate jacket, a cargo pant, a chunky hoodie, a sleeveless vest, and a sweatpant. I'd call your yellow vest, your midnight vest, and your striped vest different *colors* of the same *style*. If your yellow vest comes in S, M, L, XL, and XXL, these also count as a single *style*. However, if you decide to make a capri version of your cargo pant or add sleeves to your vest, each of these new shapes counts as an additional *style*.

— — — —

START WITH A BRAIN DUMP OF IDEAS

Back in Lesson 3, you made hand sketches of your early ideas. This got you thinking about features your ideal client might love. To get your plans flowing, the lesson asked you to choose your five favorite ideas to sketch. Perhaps, though, you had more in mind and it was tough to limit yourself. And maybe you've come up with even more ideas since then. That's okay! No one's asking you to stop having ideas. If you're like most designers and entrepreneurs, preventing ideas is nearly impossible, anyway.

That said, now's the time to get serious about your strongest styles. To this, I find it helpful to get all ideas out of your head and onto paper. So, start with a brain dump of every style you're considering. If you have 15–20 possible ideas, list them all. (It's better to shelve an idea intentionally now, than to rush this step and regret it later.)

Next, write a brief description for each. Then revisit your brand's "why." There's a reason your brand exists, and every style you choose must express it. Think about your target market and how your apparel will solve a problem for them. (Revisit the **Lesson 1** and **Lesson 2 Worksheets** as needed.)

Keep in mind: This step is about planning; your goal is to come up with a well-rounded approach to your designs. Your job is to consider the strategy of your list.

Eliminate All But Five or Fewer

After you've brain dumped all your ideas, it's time to eliminate. Let go of any styles that don't directly serve your brand's purpose. You don't have to abandon them completely or promise to never create them—keep the list somewhere for future reference. But you do have to decide which styles you're going to pursue first. Consider how much time and money you have to devote. Now that you know the steps involved, make a conscious decision about how many items to begin with. As I've mentioned, I encourage you to start with five or fewer items. For some brands, one is all they need.

As you refine your list of styles, consider a well-rounded approach. For example, if you want to make tops and bottoms and you can envision several versions of each, narrow your list to at least one top and one bottom. Unless your brand is geared toward only one type of garment, don't get carried away with planning, say, six tops, while forgetting about the bottoms.

HOW MANY STYLES DO YOU WANT TO LAUNCH WITH? WRITE A DESCRIPTIVE LIST OF THE PRODUCTS YOU ARE GOING TO DEVELOP. TO NARROW YOUR STYLES AND PLAN A WELL-ROUNDED LINE, COMPLETE **WORKSHEET 5A.**

Emma's Story

"I've seen a lot of people stop at the research step, so don't get stuck in it. It's tempting to take in all of the feedback from people and get stalled as a result. Tune in to your why at every single step. You've started this for a reason. Take in the feedback and write it down. But make sure to do the exercise of circling the ones that are relevant and crossing out the ones that aren't. Then move on. It's great to hear feedback, but don't let it bog you down. Keep moving forward with your vision.

"If you're hiring a tech designer, ask them what department they worked in in their company. If they say anything other than tech design, they probably don't have as much experience in tech writing. There are some really good tech designers that are younger, but it really depends on the program they went to and, more importantly, the portfolio they can show you. For example, a tech pack should always be at least 6 pages long. If someone shows you one that's shorter, then you don't want to hire them.

"As a DIYer, I'm always looking forward to the next step. I need to take charge and be ready with my vendors. When looking for tech designers, the next thing I'd ask is, 'Do you know a patternmaker?'"

GET A TECH SKETCH MADE

WHAT'S A TECH SKETCH?

A *tech sketch* is a professionally rendered black-and-white drawing of a garment a designer envisions. It is made on a computer and shows where seams and stitches will appear. Used early in the design process *and* in the late stage of manufacturing, a tech sketch is the most efficient way to communicate with vendors about what they'll create. Note: Because tech sketches show garments as if they were laid flat on a table, they are also known as *flat sketches*.

WHY DO I NEED IT?

A tech sketch is intended to portray a garment's shape only, so you don't need to worry about patterns or colors at this stage. What you *do* need to focus on is identifying a skilled professional to make your sketch. Hiring a tech designer is a process in and of itself. To make this as seamless as possible (ha), I've broken it into five steps. Note that the tech designer's end product will be a black-and-white digital file.

In the apparel industry, skipping this step can be commonplace. But doing so is a mistake! Having a reliable sketch can save you thousands of dollars and many headaches down the road. Soon, you'll be hiring a patternmaker, who will use the sketch as a detailed guide to turn your 2D design into a pattern made to fit a body.

Much later, when you reach your manufacturing stage, you'll include tech sketches as part of what's known as a *tech pack*. This is a collection of instructions you'll give to your factory to communicate key details about construction, stitching, sizing, and more.

STEP 1: UPDATE YOUR HAND SKETCHES AS NEEDED

Now that you've settled on the styles you plan to make, create a hand sketch for each. As you learned in Lesson 3, this is *not* the time for perfection, or even attractiveness, for that matter. Focus on the relevant details, and add notes wherever necessary to clarify your intentions and desires.

Taking time to draw your ideas forces you to find clarity about what features you want. And more importantly, you'll soon need to *show* vendors what you mean. You can never assume others will understand what's in your head. They won't.

IF YOU NEED TO DRAW SKETCHES FOR NEW DESIGNS, REVISIT **WORKSHEET 3A AND 3B** AS NEEDED.

STEP 2: GATHER INSPIRATION

A hand sketch is only part of the task. In order to show vendors what's in your head, you'll need additional visuals for inspiration. Though your hand sketches may not be professional or pretty, the inspiration you're about to gather will be. In this lesson, I define *inspiration* broadly. I'm asking you to gather visual cues that resonate with you, that will help others see what you want.

Gather whatever form is accessible and meaningful to you. Maybe you love magazines and want to clip photos that portray your vision. Perhaps you want to pull actual garments from a favorite boutique or sporting-goods store. Or maybe you'd like to build a Pinterest board.

The point is to gather things that represent the styles, textures, detailing, and brand vibe you're striving for. The more you can fully convey what you're picturing, the better. You'll use these items, along with your hand sketches, to show others soon, including your patternmaker. Having tangible, visible, real products will help you explore the specific attributes of the products you're designing and will help ensure you avoid mistakes or errors down the road.

STEP 3: GET FEEDBACK FROM YOUR TARGET MARKET

While making hand sketches and gathering inspirational visuals, it's likely you gained new insights. Did you encounter any new questions you hadn't considered before? I hope so! Gaining clarity is vital to staying motivated and increasing your chance of successfully producing your line. Your task now is to get feedback from people in your target market. Determine how you'll show your people the hand sketches and your inspirational items. Then find out what they think!

TO GET FEEDBACK FROM YOUR TARGET
MARKET, COMPLETE **WORKSHEET 5B.**

STEP 4: FIND YOUR TECH DESIGNER

Now that you've gotten feedback (and incorporated it), it's time to get tech sketches made. Seek out a tech designer with experience in your style of apparel. You don't want to hire a designer in the outdoor space to design your bridal line. The more they *get* your overall look and feel, the more accurately they'll portray your idea. Look at their portfolio. Ask questions about their past work, and have them explain their philosophy and procedure.

When it comes to hiring a tech designer, the onus is on you to do your homework. There's a wide range of quality out there. As with every vendor in this industry, you'll soon learn there's no vendor fairy. (Sigh! If I could make that happen, I would.) If you are having trouble finding a tech designer, you can search websites like Fiverr and Upwork. Or better yet, join The Apparel Mentor community and we will guide you! Remember, the apparel industry is set up to serve established companies, and not new clothing brands like you. This might take some serious digging and vetting in order to find someone that will work with you.

A solid going rate is $200–$1,000 per style. If this seems expensive, know that it's fundamental to your success. You *do not* want to have a garment produced down the road, only to discover too late that it doesn't match your vision. For one thing, that will end up costing you a lot more than the $200–$1,000 you would have spent on the tech designer—to say nothing of the labor, time, and energy lost in the process. Follow your own criteria about who you like to work with, and how. Regardless of your qualifications for a tech designer, be prepared. Ask questions, and do your part to provide clarity and a smooth relationship.

STEP 5: GET TECH SKETCHES MADE

Part of hiring a tech designer means providing them with what they'll need to understand your vision and bring it to life in their black-and-white rendering. Of course, be clear about how many garments you're making, and specify what each one is. Then, help them see what you see; this is where your hand sketches and inspirational visuals come into play. Use whatever tools you have on hand to explain what you want.

Talk to the designer about their process. Not all tech designers are the same. Some prefer to keep things straightforward and make only one sketch per garment. Others like to play a more creative role and provide two or three versions of style. In this case, your tech designer may act as a fellow visionary who can help you picture things you may not have considered.

--- --- **Mentor Moment** --- ---

Pros and Cons of Multiple Versions

How many versions of a sketch should the designer make? That's up to you (and them). There's no right or wrong approach, so listen to your gut. Perhaps you know exactly what you need, and simply want someone to draw your vision. Many designers get overwhelmed by too many ideas and will benefit from scaling back the options. In that case, request just one version.

On the other hand, maybe you're less comfortable with the design aspect, or would otherwise benefit from riffing with an expert who can show you new possibilities. In that case, it's perfectly viable to request two or three versions for each style. Regardless, provide the tech designer with everything relevant you've gathered, including your hand sketches and inspirational items.

Once you've agreed on their deliverable, make sure the terms are clear. Ensure a contract is in place that outlines how revisions work. Then, once the designer completes your sketches, look closely. Do they match what's in your head? If not, some back and forth may be required. Take the time to get this right. These documents will serve as a key communication tool going forward.

FOR A CHECKLIST OF ALL STEPS IN
GETTING TECH SKETCHES MADE,
SEE **WORKSHEET 5C.**

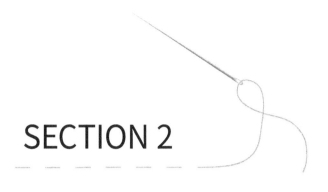

SECTION 2

FIND YOUR FABRIC

Finding your fabric—a.k.a., fabric sourcing—is just as it sounds. This section is all about finding the actual fabric you will use from the actual long-term source.

LESSON 6

UNDERSTAND FABRIC

Lesson Objectives

In this lesson, you'll gain a better understanding of fabric by:

- ► Establishing a non-retail mindset.
- ► Determining your place on my Three Tiers of Fabric Vendors chart.
- ► Distinguishing the two fabric camps: woven vs. knit.
- ► Preparing swatches for potential vendors.

Once your tech sketches are complete, you should pat yourself on the back. You've put yourself in an elite camp of new designers who choose to prioritize strategy. Thanks to your dedication, you now have a clean, professional representation of what you mean when you talk about your designs. And, if you're the type who tends to change their mind, your tech sketches can help *you* stay on track.

At this stage, many new designers get excited about fabric and can't wait to start ordering! If this is you, I share your enthusiasm. You'll get there soon, in Lesson 8. But believe it or not, sourcing fabric and trims is something you need to prepare for, especially if you're new to the apparel industry.

ESTABLISH A NON-RETAIL MINDSET

As an apparel designer, your ultimate goal is creating a style your customers love. On the other hand, as a business owner you have an equally important goal: Establishing a supply of fabric and trims that's *affordable* and *reliable*. Finding the sweet spot requires that you begin to think like a vendor. When referring to "vendors" throughout this section, I am describing sellers of raw materials such as fabric or trims that sell in bulk (not retail).

BREAK THE RETAIL HABIT

If you're like most new designers, your only encounters with fabric so far have been in a retail environment. As such, many designers fall into the rookie trap of having a retail mindset, when it comes to sourcing their materials. This habit can trip you up in many ways, so it's crucial to shift your thinking now.

For example, you probably already know that sourcing fabric means finding fabric. After all, how could you be ready to order in bulk, if you've never seen the material with your own eyes, or actually touched it? Many aspiring designers head to their local fabric store in search of fabric that looks and feels right. If this is you, stop. Turn around. Drop the swatches. Exit those automatic glass doors now. That's right! *Walk away* from the retail shop.

WHY DESIGNERS NEED VENDORS

As an apparel designer, you should work exclusively with fabric vendors that sell in bulk. Unlike retail stores that change their stock regularly, vendors operate on a larger scale and offer a regular supply. Imagine falling in love with a fabric you found at Jo-Ann, only to realize it's not available by this time next year, or even next season!

In addition, wholesale and factory direct fabrics tend to be of considerably higher quality than what's available for hobby sewists at the big-box store. If that's not enough reason for you to go to industry vendors, keep this in mind: these wholesale fabric and trims cost less per yard, since apparel designers require larger quantities than retail buyers. All of these reasons demonstrate the importance of adopting a non-retail mindset when launching your new clothing brand. Starting now, commit to avoiding retail when sourcing your fabric and trims.

THREE TIERS OF FABRIC VENDORS

In Lesson 8, you'll seek out suitable fabric vendors for your garment's materials. For now, your job is to understand what I call "Mindy's Three Tiers of Fabric Vendors." To understand the tiers, you must recognize that vendors are *not* all equal. Similarly, apparel designers *aren't all equal,* either. Like it or not, size matters, at least in our industry. The larger the buyer, the more influence they have on what they can buy, and the more options are available to them. For new clothing brands like you, it's crucial to understand where you fit on the tiers.

WHY THE TIERS MATTER

Finding the right tier is a key step. If you've ever heard the expression, "He's got champagne taste on a beer budget," then you know why this matters. When problems occur, it's not because a designer is on one tier or another. Rather, it's because their expectations are out of whack, or, at the very least, mismatched. There's nothing wrong with any of the tiers, but make no mistake: They operate differently, in fundamental ways.

The better you understand the differences among the tiers—and identify the one that's aligned to your brand and budget—the happier you'll be. (And if all goes as planned, the more profitable, too!)

TIER 1: STOCK

Of all the new designers I've worked with over the years, most fall within what I call Tier 1, or Stock. This category describes fabric vendors that hold stock of certain fabrics and colors. This is the simplest way to get fabric. You call them up, and they pull from their stock and ship it to you. Here, designers have fewer options and less power in terms of getting *precisely* what they want. They're limited to stock fabric and trims, which vendors produce in a predetermined range of fabric types.

As I've mentioned, there's nothing wrong with being on Tier 1. In fact, I find it can be a blessing for new designers, because they have enough decisions to make as it is, all while getting the hang of this industry. Generally, you'll find an abundance of fabric types (even if it's not that *exact* shade you've been dreaming about). Another advantage is that Tier 1 buyers avoid the additional time it takes to develop custom materials.

On the other hand, if a color's out of stock, it's out. The time it takes to restock is relatively set, and there's not much you can do to influence the process. Because Tier 1 materials are pre-set, their cost is relatively fixed, too, so don't expect to sweet-talk vendors into a lower price.

TIER 2: MADE TO ORDER

If you're a designer with an established brand or otherwise can afford to buy large quantities of fabrics made for your specific needs, your zone is Tier 2: Made to Order. This category describes fabric vendors that have a huge library of fabric swatches they have already developed but that do not have yardage in stock. So if you want to purchase from them, they will make your yardage per your order. Of course, even if you can afford Tier 2, you still have the option of ordering from Tier 1 stock vendors when appropriate. But for designers at this level, it can be an advantage to find more unique fabric and custom colors.

If you're a Tier 2 designer, be ready to invest more time in choosing your special fabric or trim and then waiting for it to arrive. The conversation with your vendor may feel more like a relationship and less like a transaction.

TIER 3: DEVELOP TO ORDER (FOR BIG KAHUNAS)

Is your company as big as Nike? If not, then Tier 3 probably isn't for you. In fact, in more than twenty years, I've only had one client where it made sense to order from Tier 3, the Develop to Order category. Still, it can't hurt for you to know this tier exists and understand how it works, at least at a high level. And who knows? Maybe you'll be operating at this huge scale down the road.

In the world of Tier 3 fabric vendors, the sky's the limit. Apparel companies that use these vendors define the fabric specs they'd like to see, and vendors find a way to make it happen. This where you can dream up a fabric that does not exist in the world and have the factory make something custom for you. For example, the client I've had that was in this tier wanted fabric with shea butter infused in it to soften the skin as it was worn. This did not exist at that time, so we had it developed. Working in Tier 3 requires a *lot* of financial capital in exchange for that level of control over your choices. Being able to select exactly what you want and fine-tune it to meet your needs is a luxury that translates to the quality of your products. But remember, Tier 3 requires a lot of money and influence and scale, and if you do reach this tier, make sure it *also* matches your mission and your ideal customers.

Mindy's Three Tiers of Fabric Vendors

Tier 1: Stock	Fabric & color selection is limited.
	Minimum Order Quantity is low, usually 1–60 yards.
	Fabric availability is not guaranteed in stock when you want it.
	Sourcing timeline is 1–12 weeks.
	Order timeline is 2–12 weeks.
Tier 2: Made to Order	Fabric & color selection is very broad.
	Minimum Order Quantity is higher, usually 800–1000 yards.
	Fabric availability is mostly guaranteed.
	Sourcing timeline is 10–20 weeks.
	Order timeline is 6–18 weeks.
Tier 3: Develop to Order *(the Big Kahunas)*	Fabric & color selection is endless.
	Minimum Order Quantity is very high, usually over 3000 yards.
	Fabric availability is guaranteed.
	Sourcing timeline is 6–12 months.
	Order timeline is 12–20 weeks.

REMEMBER: This chart represents *Mindy's* Three Tiers of Fabric Vendors. I named them for the sake of my own Apparel Mentor members. So *don't expect* to hear these categories used in the field. Still, they'll be valuable tools for you in your own internal processes and decisions.

HOW TO KNOW WHICH TIER A VENDOR IS IN

By now, you probably know which tier is the right fit for your brand. Going forward, own it! We've seen too many designers waste precious time and money thinking they're at a tier level that's unrealistic or second guessing themselves. We'd rather see you get comfy in your zone as soon as possible. Accepting reality will get your garment to market faster!

At this stage, you're not ready to commit to a certain vendor. Not yet. This is your time to observe the landscape of potential vendors at a high level. For now, your job is simply to identify the type of vendor you *might work with* down the road. Think of this like picking your ideal customer—someone to set your sights on and help you refine your decisions. There are plenty of fundamentals to grasp before you're ready to commit to a vendor and start working with them.

How do you know which tier a vendor is in? By asking a few key questions, you should be able to figure this out relatively quickly. For example, some things you might ask include:

- Do you stock fabric that I order from or do you make fabric per my order?
- Can I choose custom colors or do I order from a preset color selection?
- What are the Minimum Order Quantities (MOQs) of your fabric?

DISTINGUISH BETWEEN THE TWO
FABRIC CAMPS: WOVEN VS. KNIT

You've established a non-retail mindset. You've determined your place on Mindy's Three Tiers. Now, you're ready to tackle another fundamental concept: wovens versus knits. This difference is so basic that it affects every decision you'll make going forward. It determines every vendor you'll work with, at every step of the process. From here on out, I'm asking you to take a side. Yes, that's right. *Every time* you make a decision like researching a vendor or sourcing your fabric, identify yourself as Team Woven or Team Knit.

The reason this matters is these two categories of fabrics function *entirely* differently from each other. So differently, that every vendor in the chain—from the fabric seller to the pattern-maker to the manufacturer—specializes in either wovens or knits. Every vendor's skill set and machinery is geared toward woven *or* knit. Think of it like a brick mason versus a drywall contractor. You would not want to ask a drywall contractor to build you a brick wall because their tools and skills don't match. Going forward, you'll make countless decisions about which vendors are right for you. Each and every one of them is also on either Team Woven or Team Knit. Knowing where you stand is essential at this step of the process.

You don't need to know everything about woven versus knit, but here are the basics.

Characteristics of Wovens and Knits

Wovens	Knits
Usually used in dressier clothes, jeans, or outerwear.	Usually used in casual wear like yoga pants and sweatshirts.
Structured and retains shape better; has little to no stretch.	Flexible and soft and stretches a lot.
Wrinkles easier and is more durable.	Easy care and wrinkle resistant.
Yarns are woven in parallel, giving little stretch.	Yarns are knitted into loops to allow stretch.

WHEN RESEARCHING VENDORS, DO YOUR HOMEWORK

As I said, it's imperative that you figure out whether you want wovens or knits and then select a vendor to match. But here's a dirty little secret: Almost no vendors will actually *tell* you this. They may be swamped, hungry for work, or unaccustomed to new designers like you. It's entirely possible they'll take on your project, without letting you know you've gotten it wrong. And don't be surprised if a potential vendor says they work on any style of garment. Rather than taking any vendor solely at their word, I advise you to do your homework.

When researching any vendor, find out whether they specialize in wovens or knits. This includes your pattern makers, factories, fabric vendors, etc. Inquire about the brands they represent. Look at their portfolios. Ask to see examples of their work. Chances are, they work well with one fabric type and don't know squat about the other. If your design falls in the other camp, walk away. Walk away immediately and don't look back.

Working with a vendor on the other "team" can lead to disastrous results. Don't let this happen to you! Mismatched relationships can go on for longer than you'd like to believe. I implore you to be proactive and get this right, each and every time you work with someone new. Soon, you'll begin sourcing fabrics. As you do, keep Team Woven and Team Knit at the top of your mind.

Emma's Story

"There's always exceptions to the rules. It's become trendy for denim to have a bit of stretch for jeans, but they're still a woven fabric. Same for men's dress shirts. There's a little more give than normal. That's because they're adding some stretch to it, but it's still a woven fabric.

"I do have one example of going to a vendor who's on the wrong team. I work with a patternmaker, and she's great. She can do both knit and woven, but our communication got crossed. I asked for a dart out of my sports bra, which is a stretch fabric. And the pattern came back with a literal dart, like you'd put in a woven t-shirt, because that's what I'd asked for. But I was like, 'Wait, there are no darts in sports bras.' You have to pinch it out or scoop it out. It's very different the way you approach a pattern with a stretch, as opposed to a woven. It was an easy thing to fix, but if I didn't know what I was doing, I would have ended up with weird sports bras."

— — **Mentor Moment** — —

Communication Warning:
Avoid Talking to Vendors about It

And now, I'm about to give you some advice that sounds counterintuitive. Are you ready to hear it? While doing your homework and placing each vendor on one team or another, I strongly recommend that you *not discuss this designation with them*. There are a couple reasons for this.

Especially if you don't know much about fabric, the less you reveal about your knowledge (or lack of it), the better. The difference between woven and knits is so basic, that vendors will dismiss you immediately if you don't grasp it. If they sense you don't know the fundamentals of fabric, they'll sniff you out as an amateur. They won't give you the time of day. And this might happen if you start asking about the distinction between the two types of fabric.

Now, at this point you may have a question for me. You may wonder: *But Mindy, how can I navigate a key consideration with vendors without talking about it?* It's certainly a fair question.

You shouldn't have to go to design school just to have useful conversations with your vendors. My goal for you is to get familiar enough with wovens and knits to know them when you see them. Then, to communicate with vendors, use the following hack. It involves preparing swatches to determine specs. Even when you're not a fabric expert, it'll allow you to source fabric effectively without fully understanding what the fabric is. This approach will allow you to follow my precept of avoiding talking to vendors about their designations while also getting from them the information you need to make good decisions. So read on.

PREPARE SWATCHES FOR DETERMINING SPECS

FIND A GARMENT YOU LOVE, THEN CUT IT UP

The following hack is the biggest hack you get from this book! Before you can order fabric, you need to be able to *describe* what you want. Before you can *describe* what you want, you need to identify what that actually is. So, your job now is to find the kind of fabric you want. The way to do this is to go shopping! Your goal is to find a garment made of fabric that looks and feels like the one you want to create. This garment will have one single purpose: to be sacrificed. That's right. Once you find a garment that matches your criteria, you'll cut it into pieces to send to fabric vendors. These swatches will become your tool for determining specs for your fabric and trims.

━ ━ Mentor Moment ━ ━

Earlier in this lesson, I told you to avoid retail when shopping for fabric. Now, this rule still rings true: Now is *not* the time to visit fabric stores. Instead, your goal is to find an example of *wholesale or factory direct* fabric that resembles the clothing you want to produce. Where can you find such fabric? *In garments that already exist.* Yes, finding these garments requires you to shop retail, but only for the *finished product* and not the fabric itself.

Indeed, completed garments are made from non-retail fabrics. These garments are just what you need, when determining fabric specs. As you shop, consider buying from your inspiration brand. After all, they are likely to have produced pieces that resemble the fabric you'll use in your garments. You will need to buy at least one sacrificial garment for each clothing style you plan to make.

Once you've bought inspiration garments for every style of fabric in your future line, head to your workspace. Grab a pair of fabric scissors. Cut each garment into 8" x 8" pieces. Before long, you'll have multiple fabric swatches ready to send to potential fabric vendors or bring to trade shows.

HOW THIS HELPS YOU

Many savvy designers have gone before you. They've proven that formal apparel training isn't necessary for establishing a successful line. Pretty much every piece of clothing we wear was originally designed by an amateur at some point, to say nothing of the many successful new clothing brands that have come into play alongside the bigger brands. That said, you simply cannot survive in this business without communicating effectively with vendors. They specialize in various roles, and they DO know the industry.

You're about to initiate conversations with fabric vendors, in particular. You'll use your swatches to gather critical information from them, efficiently and cleanly. Even if you don't have the right words to ask for fabric specs, your homemade swatches will be your ticket to getting what you need. This is similar to creating design sketches and using inspiration pieces to convey to vendors what you're looking to create—you're providing accurate visual representations to make sure the right information is conveyed.

Sometimes the apparel industry feels like the most confusing group of professionals on the planet. But with the hack of bringing or mailing your fabric swatches to a vendor and asking if they have something similar, you will immediately get them on the same page as you. This is the standard practice in the industry, so you will also look more professional.

Mentor Moment

When I first got started, I certainly felt overwhelmed by the way the industry works. It amazed me that someone could have a great idea, all the means and money in the world, and still it would be virtually impossible to get things done without knowing this archaic crazy lingo. It's completely unstandardized, by the way! I know we've all seen examples of that first-hand. Take sizing, for one thing. I don't know about you, but when I go to Target, I'm a size large; when I go to Nordstrom, I'm a size medium; and when I go to Made Well, I'm a size small. Crazy, right?

In any case, I've often said that the apparel industry reminds me of the Wild, Wild West. It's an industry where everyone's constantly reinventing the wheel and shooting from the hip at every angle. Somehow, in all the chaos, we manage to get a few things done. And a big part of that is having *real swatches of fabric* to show to people to get our visions across. So don't forget your swatches when you head out to talk to vendors!

DON'T FORGET THE TRIMS

During this step, don't forget about the trims! These refer to embellishments that aren't fabric, such as buttons, snaps, and zippers. Trims may seem like an afterthought, especially if you're new to designing apparel. Yet in a funny way, they have the ability to *make* an outfit, all while seeming subtle.

Consequently, as you shop for inspiration garments to use for swatches, be on the lookout for trims as well. Which details make a piece feel special? Are they metal, plastic, elastic, or something else? Do any closures catch your eye? Are there strings, beads, or fringe involved? As you explore, think about your ideal customer. Consider what they care about, and ponder whether each trim might entice them to buy, or better yet, stay loyal to you afterward.

There are so many kinds of trims, it'd be impossible to name them all here. Don't get concerned about learning everything there is to know. Comprehensive knowledge isn't necessary! Instead, your role for now is to start noticing them. If you encounter a detail you especially love, buy the item and include it in your collection of inspiration garments for sourcing.

Down the road, you'll make decisions about which fabric and trims are needed. As a business owner and designer, you'll learn to balance beauty and cost. For now, put yourself in learning mode. During the sourcing process, you'll learn more about each material you've gathered. You'll also be able to start putting together source materials that will allow you to convey your intentions to potential vendors and sidestep revealing your lack of formal training in garment design while *also* demonstrating that you do indeed know what you're talking about.

Want more help? Join our community at theapparelmentor.com.

ARE YOU ON TEAM WOVEN OR KNIT? THIS MATTERS BECAUSE IT WILL CHANGE WHAT FACTORIES THAT YOU WANT TO WORK WITH. TO PREPARE TO SOURCE YOUR FABRIC AND TRIMS, COMPLETE **WORKSHEET 6.**

LESSON 7

IDENTIFY SPECS FOR YOUR FABRIC & TRIMS

Lesson Objectives

In this lesson, you'll determine the specs for all fabric and trims needed in your garment. You will:

- ► Identify essential attributes of the fabric and trims you'll order for making prototypes.
- ► Find vendors to send swatches to for purposes of determining specs.
- ► Keep a detailed record of the specs you identify, one by one, for each fabric and trim. As you go, research related jargon.

In the next lesson (Lesson 8), you'll be placing orders for fabric and trims to use in your prototypes. But here's the thing: These materials can be described in a million ways. Ours is an industry with few standards for how things should operate. When wholesalers and vendors talk about their product, they use jargon. Some of this language may be commonplace in our trade, while other terms may be unique to that company. Either way, expect to encounter unfamiliar vocabulary.

This situation may sound innocent enough, but your money and time are precious. Ordering the wrong fabric will cost you both, so let's do everything in our power to avoid communication issues. Your job is to sort through a jumble of inconsistent descriptions and identify key information. You'll use it to place your orders. Especially if you don't know the lingo, you'll rely on specs.

Short for *specifications*, "specs" refers to precise attributes of a material, such as color, weight, or size. In a world of fabric vendors who don't have time to show you the ropes, think of specs as your reliable, trusty friend. Indeed, specs will become your tool for describing exactly what you want. Use them effectively, and you'll avoid frustration, confusion, and wasted time during the sourcing process. Now, let's get started identifying specs for your fabric and trims.

IDENTIFY ESSENTIAL ATTRIBUTES OF FABRIC AND TRIMS

If I were having coffee with you and a friend, what might happen if I said, "Close your eyes and picture a green sweatshirt"? Chances are good that each of you would picture a vastly different sweatshirt, even though you're both following the same prompt. Maybe you envisioned vibrant kelly green while your friend saw a calming sage color. Maybe the necklines were different. Maybe the trims, embellishments, and other features would make those two sweatshirts seem like completely different items of clothing.

When it comes to identifying fabric and trims, keep that anecdote in mind. Fabric and trims can be described in countless ways, and your role is to identify—and later describe—the attributes of your exact material. It's not enough to just say "I want to make a green sweatshirt." You have to be *precise* about what you want, and that often involves using specific terms—and being able to identify the essential features in the first place!

Infinite possibilities of fabric and trims exist, and each material can be described in countless ways. (If you haven't already noticed this, you'll soon see a dizzying variety of approaches when vendors talk about their product.) Though it'd be impossible to categorize every single attribute in the world of apparel, we must start somewhere.

Below is a list of the essential attributes that make up each category. You'll capture these as you gather your specs. Though they aren't comprehensive, they represent the bare minimum of what you need. They'll help you compare apples to apples when evaluating pricing, for example.

ESSENTIAL ATTRIBUTES OF FABRIC AND TRIMS

To identify specs for each material you want to order, you'll first seek out a few fabric vendors whose materials may be appropriate for your project. Then, you'll provide each with an 8" x 8" swatch, cut from inspiration garments you bought. Next, you'll contact each vendor and ask them to identify the following specs. Keep detailed records as you go.

Fabric Specs: Three Key Attributes

1. **Content.** This refers to the percentage of material in your fabric. It's what appears on a garment tag, such as "97% cotton, 3% spandex."
2. **Type of Knit or Woven.** There are so many varieties of each type that it's impossible to name, or even categorize, them here. When communicating with vendors, simply ask them to tell you which type of knit or woven your chosen fabric represents.

3. **Weight.** Like type, fabric weight can be described in countless ways. Ask them to tell you what it is.

Trim Specs: Four Key Attributes

1. **Size.** Trims come in a wide variety of sizes. Ask the trim vendor to tell you what size each of yours is. Note that there's no single unit of measurement for all trims. Depending on the item, it may come in millimeters, inches, or any other designation.
2. **Color.** Find out the name that refers to the color of your item. What looks like a brass rivet to you, may be described as bronze by the vendor.
3. **Material/Quality.** Not all trims are made the same! Think of zippers. A wide-tooth plastic zipper on a sporty backpack is very different from a tight metal zipper on the back of a dress. Find out what your trim is made of, as well as any terms that describe it.
4. **Branded or Not?** Items like buttons or zippers can have a company's brand emblazoned on them. This may sound like a subtle difference, but branded trims increase the cost.

FIND VENDORS TO PROVIDE SWATCHES TO

LEARN THE LANDSCAPE

Now that you're familiar with the key components, it's time to seek out vendors who can help you determine your specs. Know that the vendors you talk to now may or may not end up being the ones you'll order from. Ultimately, you'll select based on a combination of style, budget, and reliability. But just like with every other lesson in this book and every phase of starting your own brand, it's important to have a comprehensive understanding of your options so you can make the right decisions and save time and money down the road.

Consider this your time to get to know the landscape of your fabric tier. It's a great opportunity to find out who's aligned with your brand and seems well suited to providing what you'll need in a timely manner. Look for people that you click with, especially those that provide the types of materials, styles, designs, products, and services that match your inspiration and mission.

GET OUT THERE AND MEET VENDORS

Your goal is to find vendors who can tell you the specs of your fabric and trims. As you determine who to approach, remember that only half of them will be on your Team. If you are Team Woven, do not waste time asking someone on Team Knit about your specs!

There are three main ways you can approach potential vendors:

- **Go to Fabric Trade Shows.** If you enjoy meeting people in person and have access to cities where trade shows are happening, attending these can be a great way to learn the business. Bring your fabric swatches with you, along with a physical or digital notebook. Ask vendors to tell you the key components of your swatch, and record their responses. Shows are full of stimulation, so be sure to put your notes in a place that's easy to find later! **Note:** If you are going to trade shows, read Lesson 8 before you go! You'll want to bring **Worksheet 8** with you.

- **Scour the Web.** Online, you'll have a wealth of options that may not be available at a trade show. You'll need to do more digging to find out who your best contact is within any company. Once you've found your contact, mail your swatch to them. If needed, establish a plan for when you'll follow up, to find out the specs.

- **Hire a Partner to Do This for You.** Determining specs can be time consuming. Some designers enjoy this process, but for many, it's more hassle than it's worth. If you're in the second camp, this may help you determine that you'd like to hire a full partner for your business. Or more resources are available through theapparelmentor.com.

- **Join Trade Associations.** Becoming a member of an apparel industry organization such as The Apparel Mentor (my community; theapparelmentor.com) or Seams (the leader of the "Made in America" movement; seams.org) and getting to know other members will lead you to many resources.

DO HOMEWORK ON THE JARGON

As you gather specs for your fabric and trims, you're bound to encounter some terms you've never heard. The apparel industry is rife with possibilities. There are very few standards to describe things in the same way. It's impossible to list or even categorize all the words you may encounter.

Be prepared to do some learning on your own. As you encounter jargon, find a way to make sense of it. Especially if you're a first-time designer, allow me to give you a pep talk: Take this process one step at a time! Let yourself be okay with the fact that you don't know *everything, right now.* At every step, gather enough information to make the necessary decisions. Then let the rest go. Over time, you'll look back and be amazed at how much you've discovered!

Emma's Story

"I'm working on developing a pair of joggers right now. I reached out to my fabric vendor who I've worked with for the past year, kind of with a few assumptions. I thought he'd know what kind of joggers I wanted to create. So I just sent him my content description for the jogger: mostly nylon, some spandex, a little bit of another fabric. At the same time, I asked him for an updated color card of a tank I'd made in the past.

"He sent me back six different headers. Honestly, none of them matched what I was looking for. Nothing he sent had a majority of nylon fabric in it. Instead, they were all variations of the tank fabric. I can guarantee you he was like, "I don't know exactly what you're looking for, so I'll send you what I have and we'll go from there." Ultimately what I need to do is send him a physical swatch of the fabric I'm looking for. He needs to touch and feel it to get a sense for what I'm looking for.

"Like sourcing fabrics, trims can be more complicated than you think. When I was sourcing zippers recently, I found that some are more common than others. I was making a zip-up track jacket, and I really wanted my center front to be a certain length. But when I went to source zippers, the lengths I wanted were significantly more expensive. I didn't need a huge quantity, not even 100 of them, but the cost wasn't worth it.

"So, I chose a zipper that was shorter than I originally wanted. It was only a half inch shorter, which seemed like no big deal. But as it turned out, I had to redo my entire pattern to make the zipper work. It helps to be sourcing materials and doing your patterns at the same time. That way you can be talking to your patternmaker about things like zipper length. Otherwise, it can create a whole issue."

KEEP A DETAILED RECORD OF THE SPECS YOU IDENTIFY

As you gather the specs for your fabric and trims, record it in a central location. You'll use your specs again and again in the following steps.

IS THE CONTENT IN THE LABEL ENOUGH INFORMATION WHEN FINDING YOUR FABRICS? *(PRO TIP: THE ANSWER IS NO!)* TO FIND VENDORS AND DETERMINE SPECS, COMPLETE **WORKSHEETS 7A AND 7B.**

LESSON 8

SOURCE MATERIALS & ESTIMATE COSTS

Lesson Objectives

In this lesson, you'll execute two main tasks: Source your materials and estimate your per-unit costs. These involve a series of smaller tasks, including:

- ▶ Make a list of fabric and trim vendors to explore.
- ▶ Assess their suitability.
- ▶ Decide which materials to order for your prototypes.
- ▶ Place orders and keep a record.
- ▶ Create a chart called a Bill of Materials, which provides an early estimate of your per-unit garment cost.

After you've identified specs of your fabrics (content, type and weight), your task is to order fabric and trims for making your samples. Sourcing these materials involves exploring possible fabric vendors, determining quantities, and estimating per-unit costs.

Note: Sourcing materials and finding a patternmaker are equally important. Think of Lessons 8 and 9 as companion activities to conduct simultaneously. In fact, you may want to consult your patternmaker as you source materials.

MAKE A LIST OF VENDORS TO EXPLORE

Ordering fabric and trims for your prototype is a huge lurch forward, so buckle up. As a startup, you are at a disadvantage. Especially if you're not an established brand, the industry isn't clamoring for your business. They want educated customers to keep the transactions succinct and easy. Finding fabric vendors requires savvy and grit. The sooner you adopt a mindset of learning, the more prepared you'll be to take everything in stride. If things feel unfamiliar right now, that's expected. Just keep going.

You'll start by compiling a list of suitable vendors to approach for price quotes. In Lesson 7, you talked to several vendors as you gathered specs. If you had a good experience with some of them, great. Add them to your list. But at this stage, you'll need more options. It takes a lot for the factors to line up in your favor, so don't fall in love with the first fabric you see.

TO MAKE A LIST OF VENDORS TO
EXPLORE, COMPLETE **WORKSHEET 8A.**

ASSESS VENDOR SUITABILITY

Many fabric and trim vendors avoid working with brands that make under 500 units per style. Especially if this is you, you need the right vendor more than they need you. For example, let's say you're at a trade show. If a booth rep can tell you don't know what you're talking about, they won't be too eager to work with you. This is not because they are cruel. The reasons being they make their money by selling you their fabrics; they do not make their money by educating you, which can take a lot of time. So again, do these steps and you will be more prepared and you will be an easier customer for them to work with.

To be fair, discovering a mismatch quickly *may* be a good thing. If a vendor's above your tier and there's *no way* you can hit their minimums, a conversation isn't worth your time. But in some cases, you may miss out on a fabric just because your lousy first impression killed the conversation. To prevent this, I've compiled a list of questions you should ask. Use them whether you're at a trade show, on the phone, or sending an email.

SIX QUESTIONS TO SOUND SMART WITH VENDORS

Ask vendors the following questions about potential fabrics they would sell to you:

1. **Is this fabric made to order or stock?**
   If it's stock, ask what colors it comes in. (Tier 1)
   If it's made to order, tell them what color you want.
   Use Pantone colors or a swatch you like the color of.
   (Tier 2)

2. **What's the country of origin for this fabric?**
   This will need to be printed on your labels. It'll influence pricing and perception of your brand.

3. **Do you have a continuous source from the exact same mill?**
   If the answer is no, this could cause costly quality issues.

4. **What is the timeline for receiving?**
   Many factors influence this answer, such as transportation method, labor supply, inter-government regulations, etc.

5. **What is the price per yard or meter?**
   This question relates to the next one. Note that you should *not* start with these. They can trigger vendors to see you as an amateur.

6. **What are your MOQs (Minimum Order Quantity)?**
   Now, here is where you must be savvy! As a new clothing brand, this question is critical. The answer tells you what tier the vendor is in. If you don't match, it's over. That said, I've placed this question last on your list. I'm intentional about this, and you should be, too. Especially if you love their fabric, you want to find out more, before having your conversation cut short. Even if they *are* in your tier, you must come across as informed, kind, and appealing to work with.

   OPTIONAL: What are the features?
   Here, you're looking for things that will help with your marketing and brand vision, such as antimicrobial, wicking, organic, and so on.

   OPTIONAL: How much do I have to order to start getting a price break?
   The higher your budget and quantity, the easier of a time you may have with this step.

Request Headers & Narrow Your Options

Let's say you go to a show and come across five to ten fabrics you like. You'll want to request *headers*, which are 8" x 8" fabric samples from the vendor. Ask for headers for them all. Typically, you'll receive them in the mail. After you get home, you'll be able to compare apples to apples. You'll be able to see how the fabrics really feel, what the color looks like in natural lighting, and how they compare to each other.

Armed with the fabric specs you've been gathering, you'll have a solid record of what's what. Your specs should be organized enough to show which vendor provided what fabric, and what each costs. If you already have a patternmaker or another expert in the industry, show them your headers. (To find a patternmaker, see Lesson 9.) These specialists can help you narrow the choices.

Sometimes, designers go to a trade show and fall in love with a fabric on the spot. I'm not saying you can't order your prototype yardage then and there. Only you know your business and budget. If you *know* you want to try the fabric, buying 10 yards may be worth the investment. Just make sure you've asked the six questions in this lesson. Know what you're getting into. The biggest thing to remember is buying sample yardage (usually 10 yards) of fabric you love is the smartest thing to do. Definitely do not purchase in bulk without prototyping in the fabric first and testing it.

TO ASK THESE SIX QUESTIONS AND
REQUEST A HEADER, COMPLETE
WORKSHEET 8B.

— — **Mentor Moment** — —

It's Like Painting a Room

Think of sourcing your fabric this way. Have you ever painted a room in your house? If so, your first step was to sort through the paint cards at the big-box home store. You know the ones: Racks and racks of cards with several shades, each just a tiny bit darker than the one before. The possibilities are endless! At this stage, everything seems fun and exciting, if overwhelming. Chances are, you've already picked some favorites before you leave the store.

Then you come home. You take out each card and hold it to the wall. Here, you can see how the light falls at different times of day. You evaluate how each shade looks when placed right next to your trim, shower curtain, or towel. More often than not, you become shocked to discover the shade you thought was perfect—a mere half hour before—suddenly bums you out. Instead, a different color rises to the top of your list.

Okay, now you have an important choice to make: Paint a few test patches or pick a winner and jump right in? Several factors influence this decision, of course: How big is the room? Who'll do the work? How expensive is your paint? What's your tolerance for risk? You know yourself best, so the choice is up to you.

But here's the thing: Skipping steps can and *will* cost you. A friend of mine once fell in love with a gorgeous slate blue that was perfect for the gray-and-white accessories she'd bought for her new bathroom. The subtle hue was just right for the calming vibe she'd create, like living in a spa. The color looked **amazing,** both at the store and on the card she briefly shoved under the wood trim of her new bathroom. "No need for test samples," she thought. "This nails it!"

It wasn't until she painted the whole damn room that a painful reality sunk in: Her classy slate had somehow become a sugary robin's egg. Surrounded, she felt a sensation that was considerably less *resort* and more, well, *nursery.* My friend was 45, a business owner with no children or plans to have any. As she stood in her bathroom, breathing fumes that had dominated her life for two days straight, she could almost hear her bathroom speak. "When's the baby coming?" It wanted to know.

She tried to convince herself the color wasn't *wrong,* per se. Instead, it was chipper and fun! "I could use more fun in my life, right?" she said weakly, under her breath. The thought of starting over was demoralizing. She had a business to run, and this project had set her back on client work. Determined this wasn't a mistake, she browsed online, searching for excuses to buy kicky new accessories to suit her bright young walls.

In the end, though, no amount of optimism was enough to cover the reality. She hated the color. It simply wasn't right. Not for a space used every day for years to come. And she couldn't help it: Each time she looked at the walls, she thought, "I'd love them . . . if only they were slate blue." Three days later, she trudged back to The Home Depot.

This time, she'd learned a lesson. She bought three sample-sized tubs, ready for the test blobs she was about to paint next to the mirror. She cued up several podcasts and devoted the next weekend to painting. Now, she loves that bathroom! She never gets tired of its classy feel. When Christmas rolled around, her boyfriend got her a white robe to hang on shower hook—perfect for her homemade spa. This is why I want you to buy only test amounts of fabric, then prototype in it before committing to bulk yardage.

DECIDE ON YOUR MATERIALS, PLACE ORDERS, AND KEEP A RECORD

Looking at headers and reviewing answers to the six questions will give you a good sense of what to order. Still, think through each piece one at a time. Look at all the information you've gathered. Then consider three factors: style, budget, and reliability. Think about the short-term goals for your prototype and the long-term goals for ordering in bulk. If you need to, take notes to sort out your thoughts. Then decide what to order for your prototypes.

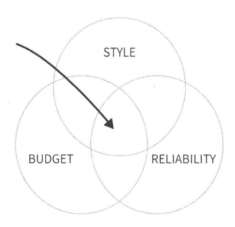

As you source your fabric, think of my friend and her spa bath. Sure, everything turned out okay in the end. But skipping the prototype stage was a mistake. Though it had seemed like a shortcut initially, this decision actually *doubled* both her cost and her time. That's not counting the frustration factor and the opportunity cost of client work she lost while needlessly repainting.

Think of your prototype, or *sample*, this same way. It's a necessary test run for every fabric and trim. (See Lessons 12–14 for making prototypes.) Now, at the sourcing stage, your goal is twofold:

- **Short term:** Order enough to make a prototype for each garment (about 10 yards for each), and no more

- **Long term:** Order only from vendors who suitably align with you in the key ways previously discussed:
  - » Tier level matches your business
  - » Style is right for your ideal customer and brand vision
  - » Price per yard or meter meets your budget
  - » Timeline meets your launch plan
  - » Has continuous supply from the same mill
  - » Country of origin suits your brand
  - » Minimum Order Quantities (MOQ) meet your needs and budget

— — **Mentor Moment** — —

A Note about Color

Painting a room is a great metaphor for why you don't want to skip prototyping. Yet unlike painting, making apparel is about *so much more than color*. When you make yours, you'll find out how the garment is going to look, feel, drape, move, and act. In fact, when it comes to it, these elements are more important than color. There's also another key difference: As a new clothing brand buying wholesale fabric, you simply don't have as many options as a consumer buying house paint. Sometimes, you have to accept your second or third choice.

Let's say you've identified a suitable vendor whose fabric you like, but they say, "The color you've requested won't be available for three months." If you are at the prototyping stage, you may have no choice but to make the sample in another color. Making a prototype can easily take three months or more, so by the time the color's ready, you'll have a lot of information about the way the garment will function.

Yard or Meter?

When ordering fabric, some vendors measure in **yards**. Some use **meters**. Country of origin plays a factor, so even if you're used to only one term or other, it's on you to learn. There are plenty of tools available to make these calculations for you. Find your favorite one and rely on it. If you're not used to these conversions now, get used to it. Over time, it'll feel second nature.

Emma's Story

"I used to work with a fabric vendor out of Portland. I never asked if they were a mill, because I knew that they weren't. But I assumed I was getting a continuous source. Turns out the assumption was wrong, and I'm not sure that they would have told me otherwise. Every single time I ordered the black fabric for my leggings, it always came back different. I definitely ordered the same one correctly; I had the style number and everything.

"But sometimes the fabric would come in and the stretch was different. The structure was so different that if I made an order and delivered it to clients, they literally had to give the leggings back to me because the fabric was so bad. And I had already tested these pants plenty of times before. So, as things ended up, I will never use that fabric vendor again because of that experience. This is why it's best to ask if this is a continuous source of the exact same fabric.

"Don't substitute fabrics when you're in the sampling process. Say you used a certain fabric in round one of your prototype, then ran out because you hadn't ordered enough. If you say, "Oh, shoot, I don't want to wait for my fabric to get here. I'll do round 2 with this other fabric. It's close enough." Don't substitute it. Go order more fabric. Get enough of it this time and *then* complete the sampling process."

TO DECIDE WHAT TO ORDER FOR YOUR PROTOTYPES, PLACE ORDERS, AND KEEP A RECORD, FILL OUT **WORKSHEETS 8C AND 8D.**

ESTIMATE YOUR PER-UNIT COSTS

START YOUR BILL OF MATERIALS (BOM)

Now that you've chosen materials for your prototype, you can start estimating your manufacturing costs. A Bill of Materials, or BOM, is a spreadsheet used to calculate *total manufacturing costs per unit.* This comes down to two main categories:

- Materials
- Labor

This is a living document that you'll update throughout the process. For now, you do know how much your *materials* will cost, at least in this current iteration. Note that these materials may change down the road, after you conduct your prototyping. Maybe you'll decide to swap out the fabric for one of your garments, in which case you'll update your BOM at that time.

Your *labor costs* won't be known until you find a factory. Generally, this occurs later in the process. In this book, it happens in Lesson 18: Choose Your Factory. For now, you can do some preliminary research and plug in an estimated labor cost. Or you can leave it blank, knowing you'll fill it in later.

A column in the BOM refers to *yield.* (For more on yield, see Lesson 16: Grade Your Pattern.) This number will also be unknown to you until you reach the factory. This refers to the amount of fabric you'll use, on average, per garment. This figure is calculated after a specialist determines how to cut your fabric in a highly engineered way (specific to your patterns), to maximize efficiency and prevent waste. Much like labor, you can do some early homework to estimate yields. Or you can leave this blank for now.

Either way, now is the time to think about all the categories of costs this project will incur.

Note: The BOM *does not* include development costs, such as hiring patternmakers, sewers, or project-management partners.

TO START YOUR BILL OF MATERIALS
(BOM), SEE **WORKSHEET 8E.**

SECTION 3

DEVELOP YOUR SAMPLES

In this section, we talk about all the necessary steps to get your samples made prior to manufacturing.

Lesson 9. Find Your Patternmaker
Lesson 10. Select Your Prototype Sewer
Lesson 11. Estimate Your Launch Dates
Lesson 12. Evaluate Your First Prototype

LESSON 9

FIND YOUR PATTERNMAKER

Lesson Objectives

To hire a patternmaker, you'll:

- ▶ Learn more about patterns and patternmakers and why you need them.
- ▶ Find potential patternmakers and ask key questions to evaluate them.
- ▶ Set your base size and take body measurements for it.
- ▶ Hire a patternmaker and equip them for the project by providing necessary information.

In this lesson, you'll find your patternmaker. This task happens while you're choosing your fabric and trims. In other words, you should do Lessons 8 and 9 at the same time. These, along with Lessons 10 and 11, prepare you for the huge milestone of making your first prototype. You'll make this prototype and evaluate it in Lesson 12. Between now and then you'll assemble the right team to make it happen.

The team members you're about to hire, including patternmakers and sewers, are highly skilled. One thing that angers me is seeing how often these professionals are undervalued. Especially if you're new to clothing design, you may be facing some old-school perceptions that crept in without your knowing it. Now, you can replace them with actionable steps for finding experienced patternmakers and asking targeted questions to evaluate their suitability for your project.

WHAT IS A PATTERN?

As I've mentioned, people become apparel designers for a variety of reasons. In my Apparel Mentoring, I see a wide range of experience: in clothing design, in running a business, and everything in between. If you don't yet know what a pattern is, it's imperative to build some fundamentals. You don't need to get caught in the weeds of every detail—that's the patternmaker's job—but you've got to know what you're hiring them to make.

The best way to do this is to take 30 seconds and search *patternmaker* on YouTube. (Go ahead and do it now. No problem. I'll wait.) Watch a video or two of these specialists in action.

As you can see, a *pattern* is a collection of 2D shapes that are traced onto fabric before being cut and assembled together, to fit a human body. Usually made of paper, patterns are designed for repeated use.

WHY IS A GOOD PATTERNMAKER IMPORTANT?

Fit is everything. It can make or break your brand. Sure, fabric is important too. But you can have the perfect fabric on an ill-fitting garment, and you will fail. The patternmaker is not the place to skimp, because this is the person who's engineering your pieces together. They bring your idea to life in a way that looks and feels right. Their creative yet technical work factors in countless adjustments to fit your target customer and deliver sizes that can be mass produced. They know how different fabrics function and calculate how much is needed. Their precise design saves you money while realizing your creative vision.

— — **Mentor Moment** — —

Rage with Me

If you hear somebody talk about an engineer, everybody listening assumes science, math, and complex thinking are involved. The role is respected and generally thought of as successful. Say the word *patternmaker*, though, and you'll get a mixed bag. Most have no clue what's even meant by the role. At least half picture a hobbyist whose leisure project may or may not be worthy of pay. In general, people aren't aware that making clothes requires deep technical knowledge *and* artistry.

As an apparel startup, I'm calling you to join me in changing outdated perceptions of our industry. At every opportunity, it's our job to help people see that patternmaking IS engineering. Just like a machinist, a patternmaker solves intricate problems. They invent, design, build, and test. In fact, I'd argue that patternmaking can be harder than developing, say, a metal part that keeps its shape. It's no small feat to create something that stretches in infinite directions.

— — — —

FIND POTENTIAL PATTERNMAKERS

There's no magic bullet for finding patternmakers. Ask around. Cast a wide net. Not every patternmaker will be right for your job, which is why you'll be asking targeted questions to evaluate them. Here are a few ideas to get you started:

- Ask a friend in the business.

- If you've secured any fabric or trim vendors, ask for their recommendations.
- Ask a factory who they recommend.
- Check out YouTube, Twitter, LinkedIn, Facebook, blogs, or other social media to see who's talking about pattern making.
- Search for podcasts on related topics.
- Seek out local, regional, or national businesses or organizations that know clothing design, such as theapparelmentor.com or seams.org.
- Talk to someone at an inspiration brand.
- Attend trade shows and ask around.
- If you're working with a full partner, depend on them to pair you.

VET POTENTIAL PATTERNMAKERS

I won't sugarcoat it: This task is challenging. Your pattern-maker is one of the most important, if not *the* most important person you're going to invite onto your project's team of vendors. This is one professional you don't want to skimp on. As tempting as it may be, don't hire somebody fresh out of college. Keep in mind that making a rushed decision on this can and will make a designer lose months. It's much more costly to redo this critical work, than to hire a pro in the first place.

COMMON PITFALLS FOR APPAREL STARTUPS

- Hiring a tailor or other professional who has never made a production pattern (designed to make multiples)

- Hiring someone from the wrong fabric team (woven or knit). They think if they're a good patternmaker, they can do a great job with every type of fabric. They may be hungry for work or overshooting.
- Thinking you need to be in the same location as your patternmaker. You might think you need to physically be there to work with them. But open your mind. Better to find someone who specializes in what you need, than limiting yourself to someone in your area.

ASK KEY QUESTIONS

Once you've made a list of potential patternmakers, be sure to ask them these key questions.

1. Approximately how many production patterns have you made? Is this your full-time job?

You are looking for a patternmaker who's *full-time job* is doing work for factories. Ideally, you'll find someone who's made over 1,000. That's a master patternmaker. Someone who's made 100 patterns could be sufficient, and the absolute minimum should be 50. If anyone's made fewer than 50, I'd consider them *not* a great patternmaker.

A key term in this question is *production patterns*. A big mistake I see is designers going to a local tailor and hiring them to do the work. Or, they hire someone just out of design school, or otherwise doing this as a side gig. When the fabric gets put together, it ends up looking really wacky. I've heard a million stories of frustrated designers who tried to save money by hiring side hustlers. As tempting as it sounds to pay the person less, you'll get frustrated as you wait for months for your project to get done. Worse, you'll have to redo the work later when the prototype ends up looking and fitting wonky.

Avoid asking potential vendors how long they've been making patterns. They could easily say *five years,* when in reality, they've only made one pattern a year. A red flag is someone who's made only 5 patterns.

2. What types of products do you have experience patterning in? (Make sure they are Team Woven or Team Knit.)

I repeat, they *must* have experience on the fabric you're working with: woven or knit. A challenge you'll face is that they won't always disclose this. And there are some out there who can do both. But generally, they have specialized in one or the other. If you really want to have the best pattern ever, you want to have somebody who specializes in your fabric type.

3. What is your pricing?

You're about to engage in business, so of course you want to understand their pricing. A patternmaker is not the place to skimp. You're hiring a professional engineer, and service from a good one is worth the price. Expect to pay roughly $500 per base pattern, depending how complicated the design is. Ranges can be anywhere from $300 to $1,000 each.

4. What's your time frame?

A typical time frame is one to four weeks. Again, make sure this isn't their side hustle.

5. Can you grade patterns?

They need to know how to make various sizes, which is called *grading*. Though you're not making other sizes yet, you're asking for them later. To find out more about grading, see Lesson 16: Grade Your Pattern.

6. Do you use ASTM standards for clothing sizes?

(In other words, are you familiar with standard terms for sizing, based on body-measurement data for the public?) Your pattern-maker should know these standards. No need to get caught in the weeds, but this refers to the American Society for Testing & Materials. This group provides data about body measure-ments that are typical for different size designations, such as husky or petite. For example, the bust, waist, hips, and sleeve should generally be X long, depending on the size category.

7. Do you pattern digitally or by hand?

The more you know about what you'll be getting, the better. I prefer digital patterns, but I wouldn't discount a patternmaker who does it by hand, just for this. (There are places that will digitize a pattern for you, if you need this done later.)

8. BONUS: Do you sew the samples? If not, do you work with a sample sewer or have one to recommend?

If you find a patternmaker who also sews samples, major bonus! You've just saved a major step! Also, communication between the patternmaker and sewer is critical. When making proto-types, you must serve as the go-between. This is tricky enough if you're new to the industry, but it's especially difficult if you and a vendor speak different languages.

TO FIND POTENTIAL PATTERNMAKERS
AND VET THEM, COMPLETE
WORKSHEETS 9A AND 9B.

SET YOUR BASE SIZE

Ultimately, you'll carry multiple sizes. For now, you'll start with what's known as your base. The base size is important because it's what you'll use to develop your prototype. During prototyping, you'll tinker until the base size fits just right. Only then, after your prototype is complete, will you have your patterns made into additional sizes.

If you're unfamiliar with apparel design, you may think coming up with sizes is a no-brainer. But in fact, you'll make a few intentional decisions. Choose carefully, because sizing affects how a customer feels when buying and wearing your clothes.

Your sizes say a lot about who your brand is. For example, have you ever seen a pair of jeans labeled size 0? If so, you're probably a woman, and the company was trying to help you feel skinnier. A move like this certainly generates opinions. While many customers may want to feel as light as air, I find it insulting to imply that women should be literally weightless. For women, sizing across brands and stores has varied widely for a long time. But this phenomenon is starting to happen more in menswear, too.

STEP 1: TAKE MEASUREMENTS
FOR YOUR IDEAL CLIENT

In Lesson 2, you explored your ideal client and what makes them tick. Now, it's time to get down to brass tacks. You must determine their measurements. Remember, this is not about making a custom outfit for you; it's about choosing a size that will generally fit your ideal customer. You should have ready access to a person that size, so they can easily try on and test your prototype as it progresses. Note: This can be you or someone close to you.

Granted, it's possible you got into this business to help a problem that you personally have. In that case, perhaps your measurements *do* represent your customer. Regardless, now is the time to identify the person who best represents your ideal customer. The goal of this step ***is not*** to say these exact measurements limit who can wear your clothes or not. Instead, the base measurements serve as a point of reference and communication tool throughout the prototyping process.

- When you're ready, record the following measurements for that individual you've selected to represent your ideal client:

TOPS	BOTTOMS
Chest:	Waist:
Waist:	Hip:
	Thigh:

If you've never taken measurements before, you'll need a special type of measuring tape for sewing. Unlike metal measuring tapes, this kind is flexible and can be wrapped around a body. The fastest way to learn is to Google "how to take body measurements." Note that the only ones you'll need for the pattern are the ones listed above for tops and bottoms. (Although tailors take additional measurements, like forearms, these are too specific for a pattern for clothing that many people will wear.)

How Inspiration Brands Can Help

Back in Lesson 2, you picked a brand to follow as inspiration. You can always go back to this as a starting point, and now is no exception. Look up your inspiration brand's sizing chart. Try on their clothes. If you like the way they do things, there's no need to reinvent the wheel. Feel free to use their sizes. But if your "why" is specific to body shape, like making clothes for pear-shaped people who don't have many options, then inspiration brands specifically won't meet your needs. Either way, they serve as a clear guide for what *not* to do. Whatever you do, make an intentional choice!

STEP 2: NAME THE SIZE

While that first step was mostly objective in nature, this next step is subjective: You must name your sizes. Companies in our industry vary widely when it comes to how they do this, and it's up to you as the business owner to decide what works for your brand. Although the ASTM has defined what's appropriate for various segments of the general population, there's no set way to go about this.

As you name your sizing, do the following:

- **Consider your brand's image.** What does your brand say about the people who'll wear it? How do

you want buyers to feel when wearing your clothes?
How will this impact sizing?

- **Try on clothes from a brand that inspires you.**
  Do you like the way they've assigned sizing? Do
  you think they got it right? If not, what would you
  change and why?

- **Name your base size.** Your base size could be a letter
  like S, M, or L. Or it could be a number like 4, 10, or
  16. This is an important decision, so be intentional.

- **Feel free to start planning future sizes, but until
  your prototype is done, focus on your base.**
  Generally, brands cover a span of five sizes, with the
  base in the middle. Especially if this is your first time
  making a prototype, remember that getting your
  base prototype right will take time and could involve
  several reiterations, developed over several months.
  Only after that's done will you make the other sizes.

TO SET YOUR BASE SIZE, COMPLETE
WORKSHEET 9C.

Emma's Story

"When you set your base size, inspiration brands can
be a great example of what to do, or what not to do.
When I was shopping for competitors for my yoga line, I
went to Lululemon and Athleta. I found that I really liked
Athleta's sizing more. They are in the S, M, L category,
versus numerical sizes. I started trying on pants and
noticing how I feel in Lululemon versus Athleta. I really

loved that when I wore Athleta, I was a size small. I felt less comfortable about the fact that in Lululemon, I was a size 10.

"As an apparel designer, I'm especially aware of how a size can make a customer *feel*. When companies like Lululemon and Athleta choose their fit designations, it's intentional. That is one hundred percent a brand decision for them. In the same way, sizing is a big part of your branding decision.

"I also have a story about how things can go wrong if you hire a side-hustler as opposed to a specialized vendor. I do all the pattern work for my company. I've made over 100 patterns, but this doesn't mean I'm the right person to make them for other brands. I'm speaking from a very personal experience, because I did this as a patternmaker, and I've seen what can go wrong. When I first launched my clothing company, other startups saw this and asked if I could do their patterns as well.

"Being an entrepreneur, I loved the idea of helping other entrepreneurs. So I said to one of them, "Yes. Let me help you build your brand." They already had fabric sourced, so they needed help getting ready for production. Ultimately, I took on *way* too much. I couldn't run my business and do a client's patterns at the same time.

"As much as I wanted to help this new brand, it was my side hustle. There was no way I could give it the focus it deserved. Fortunately, this was with one client and it was a friend, so I was able to back out of the situation gracefully. Be wary of people who aren't doing pattern-making as their main job. You probably won't be paying them as much, which may sound intriguing. But it's going to take longer, and they won't have the dedication and experience you're looking for. Instead, find someone who's doing pattern engineering as their main gig."

HIRE YOUR PATTERNMAKER

You've evaluated potential patternmakers to determine who is suitable. You've established your base size. Now it's time to get started and hire this important vendor! To ensure a successful experience, make sure they understand your project fully.

It's up to you to be easy to work with. As with every vendor at every stage of the process, you must be proactive and organized. Communicate what you want clearly, in a mutually respectful way. Remember, this industry is not kind to those who waste vendors' time.

And, like every task you conduct as a business owner, you need to do your due diligence. Although this book isn't geared toward teaching business law, make sure you understand the contract. Ensure a shared understanding about things like process and payment. Clarify who owns the copyright, and get it in writing. This is a valuable asset, and if you don't own the pattern, you can get trapped by limitations down the road.

WHAT TO PROVIDE

Patternmakers are skilled professionals, but they can't read your mind. When you hire them, provide the following:

- **Your tech sketches.**
- **Body measurements.**
- **A swatch of your fabric.** Or, if they're sewing your sample, then send the quantity they need.
- **Inspiration images.** Give them access to any files you have showing the look, feel, and fit you envision.
- **Inspiration garment.** Make an effort to provide an actual garment that fits how you want it to. *Do not*

skip this step. Doing it can help eliminate the number of samples the patternmaker will have to make.

Mentor Moment

TIP: Your patternmaker does *not* need to live in your area. Instead, it's more important to find a skilled engineer. You can have a perfectly useful conversation with this vendor online, so they don't have to live down the street.

TO HIRE YOUR PATTERNMAKER, COMPLETE **WORKSHEET 9D.**

LESSON 10

SELECT YOUR PROTOTYPE SEWER

Lesson Objectives

In this lesson, you will:

- ► Find potential sewers.
- ► Evaluate their suitability for your project.
- ► Equip them by providing necessary information.

FROM DESIGN TO PROTOTYPE

If you've completed your pattern, congratulations! You've successfully navigated the first phase of turning your apparel idea into a saleable product. Now that you've articulated your design (Phase 1), you're about to make your prototype (Phase 2). Soon you'll see your design come to life, in all its 3D glory.

Getting the early versions right doesn't happen by accident. It's your job to assemble a committed, skilled team. In this lesson, you'll find one of your most important roles: the sewer for your prototype.

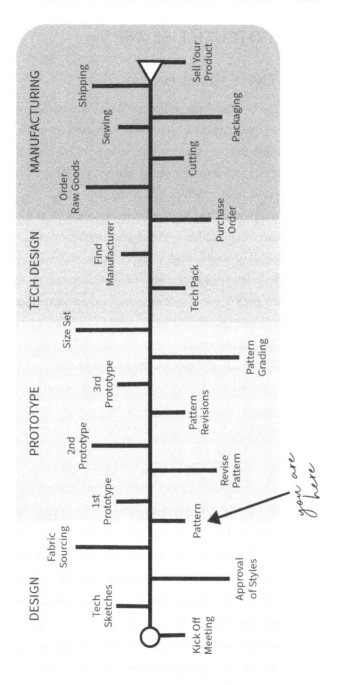

PRODUCTION TIMELINE

DESIGN

Tech Sketches
Kick Off Meeting
Fabric Sourcing
Approval of Styles

PROTOTYPE

1st Prototype
Pattern
2nd Prototype
Revise Pattern
3rd Prototype
Pattern Revisions
Size Set
Pattern Grading

TECH DESIGN

Find Manufacturer
Tech Pack
Purchase Order

MANUFACTURING

Order Raw Goods
Sewing
Shipping
Cutting
Packaging
Sell Your Product

you are here

FIND POTENTIAL SEWERS

CHALLENGES YOU'LL FACE

Finding a sewer for your prototype is no joke. Indeed, this step alone takes grit and creativity. There's a reason we dedicated an entire lesson to it, so don't get discouraged if this step takes you some time. In an industry of big players, you're at a disadvantage if you're new, small, or unknown.

In many ways, the apparel industry operates as an underground network, hidden to those who aren't part of it. Apparel professionals generally work with people they already know. As a new designer, your task is to find your way into an environment that *isn't* known for consistency, infrastructure, or transparency. While this challenge can apply to any apparel role, it's especially true for sewers.

Finally, finding a prototype sewer is challenging because you must weed out individuals who make one-offs, but have no production experience. As with your patternmaker, it's not good enough to hire a local tailor or other sewing side gigger. It's critical to seek out professionals with production experience. Their full-time job needs to be sewing for factories.

If there's one thing I want you to get from this lesson, it's this: Avoid hiring a tailor or seamstress, at all costs. Making a garment for an individual takes an impressive level of mastery, but *it's not the same thing* as making a prototype for the masses. Your pieces will be produced over and over again, which requires a development process designed for maximum efficiency.

I can't tell you how many times I've seen startup owners make the mistake of thinking all sewers are equal. Probably like you, they drive by alteration shops all the time. They

Google *tailor* and instantly find options. Or they have a friend of a friend who loves to sew clothes. Not knowing what they're getting into, these new designers get tempted by the ease of finding a nearby sewer who's willing to work for a bargain. Do not fall into this trap! Sooner or later, it will cost you.

HARD WORK, LOW PAY, AND LANGUAGE BARRIERS

By now I hope I've convinced you it's worth your time to find the right kind of sewer for your product. You must go on the hunt for a production sewer. They won't be easy to find, but your scrappiness will be rewarded.

Prototype sewers are in high demand and have little time for those who don't know the industry. Many startup owners don't sew. If this is you, you probably have an inaccurate perception of what sewers are like. First, it's important to understand that production sewers are valuable specialists, and they know things you don't. And even though they're the hardest working professionals in the industry, they tend to be the lowest paid.

Production sewers don't make money by teaching the ropes to startups like you. Their schedules are too demanding as it is. It's also important to know that sewers often come from immigrant populations. If you're not part of a vendor's community, you need to work hard to discover and build relationships.

As in any situations where collaborators speak different primary languages, expect all interactions to take longer. I've seen it time and time again: Patient designers fare far better than those who try to rush the process.

MUTUAL RESPECT AND LIKEABILITY

When seeking your sewer, never underestimate the value of mutual respect. Likeability takes you far. In short, don't be a jerk. Do your homework on things you don't understand. Listen, learn, and make life easier for any potential sewer you interview. Never forget that production sewers have choices. Their skills are rare, they're in high demand, and you need them more than they need you.

When I've seen startups succeed, it's because they were scrappy and found this underground world. They took the time to build an awesome partnership with their sewer. Sewers have to *want* to work for you. If they mess up, it's generally a misunderstanding. Instead of getting mad, think about how you can contribute to a long-term relationship. Not only will they be happier, but it turns into a direct benefit for your business. (This assumes you've vetted them first with the questions in **Worksheet 10b**, and you know they're professional.)

ASK YOUR PATTERNMAKER FOR RECOMMENDATIONS

As you'll experience, finding potential sewers is a process. To streamline it, start with any trusted connections you've already developed. For example, your patternmaker may have sewers to recommend. If you haven't already done so, ask. If they say yes, you're in luck.

If you had a good experience with your patternmaker and have faith in their credibility, chances are their sewer will be equally dependable. Even so, always do your homework and vet the person yourself.

CHECK WITH A MANUFACTURER

Not all patternmakers have sewers to recommend. For many designers, more digging will be required. Another place to seek out production sewers is your manufacturer. If you have one, reach out and ask for recommendations. If you don't have a factory yet, don't panic. In fact, if you're thinking that this book hasn't even addressed the topic of finding a manufacturer yet, you're right!

Finding a manufacturer is another *process,* in and of itself. Because it can seem convoluted, I'm holding off on that till Lesson 18, *after* you've completed prototyping and tech design. That said, it's possible you may have stumbled across a potential manufacturer or two. Or maybe this isn't your first attempt at making your line, and you've already found your manufacturer.

If you do have a manufacturer, reach out. Find out more about their sewers. Could they be hired to make your prototype? Do they work on site, or from their homes? Can you visit the floor to get a sense for how it works?

CONTINUE SEARCHING ON YOUR OWN

As great as it sounds to find a sewer through your patternmaker or manufacturer, this isn't always possible. In fact, it's a rarity. The reality is that most new designers will need to do some digging.

Your goal is to find a production sewer, often called a *sample sewer,* who specializes in the type of garment you're making and has experience with manufacturers. As you embark on your search, get ready to cast a wide net. Be creative. And get ready to talk to people! Keep in mind many sewers don't have fancy websites or social media. Their focus tends to be sewing, not marketing.

With your goal in mind, make a list all the possible places you might look:

- Attend trade shows and ask around.
- Ask a friend in the business. Or friends/family who love networking and can stretch you past your immediate contacts.
- Ask vendors or a factory who they recommend.
- Check out YouTube, Twitter, LinkedIn, Facebook, blogs, or other social media for people making samples.
- Search for podcasts on related topics.
- Seek out local, regional, or national businesses or organizations that know clothing design.
- Talk to someone at an inspiration brand.
- Visit boutiques or international marketplaces where clothing is made in large quantities. Ask the proprietor.
- If you're working with a full partner, they should have you covered with production sewers.
- Keep coming up with creative ideas of your own.

As you search, it's possible you'll find more than one option. This is a good thing! Because sewers are in such high demand, it's not unusual for them to drop out, even after you thought a relationship was secure. It's better to err on the side of too many options, rather than not enough.

TO FIND POTENTIAL SEWERS,
SEE IDEAS IN **WORKSHEET 10A.**

VET POTENTIAL SEWERS

If you've made it to this step, nice work! This means you've gathered one or more potential sewers. Now it's time to assess their suitability for your project. You'll do this by asking some key questions. I compiled them after seeing too many startup owners hit pitfalls of not vetting this important vendor. I put them in order of importance, so *you should ask them in the same order as they appear on the worksheet.*

After all, it's your business. It's your product. You are the project manager, and you're the one responsible for your ultimate quality, process, and budget.

ASK KEY QUESTIONS

1. Approximately how many production prototypes have you sewn?

There's a difference between production sewers and tailors/ seamstresses who make one-off garments. Ensure they have experience with manufacturers. This should be their full-time job. It's important to distinguish the difference; a tailor is probably one person moving through all the different machines, whereas a production team is usually two to five different sewers stationed at different machines repeatedly sewing, the same thing, efficiently and accurately every single time.

2. What percentage of your work is wovens vs. knits?

Be wary of sewers who claim to do it all. (This is common!) They must specialize in your fabric type. If you don't see a high percentage (say, 70%) of garments in your type, move on. If you hire the wrong vendor, your prototype will come back looking really . . . bad.

Let's say you find a vendor who's used to sewing woven trousers, dress shirts, and blazers, and you bring them a yoga pant that is stretchy and has lots of compression. They might give it back to you falling apart, with stitches popping, and you wouldn't even be able to wear it.

3. Show me examples of your work.

Their pieces should look good enough to hang in a store. Even if you're new, follow your intuition. If the shapes look off, they won't work for the manufacturer.

4. How do you work? What do you need to make this a success?

Some do their own cutting, for example. Others don't, and you'll have to find a cutter too. Find out their needs, and help however you can. Know exactly what you need to come to them with in order for them to sew your product.

5. What's your time frame?

The typical time is 1–4 weeks. If the person's language is new to you, consider padding this by 1–2 weeks. And if there is a delay or you're sensing a delay, you can always ask point blank, "What are you missing?" You may be able to speed up sample time by using digital prototyping, if that is an option with your product.

6. What's your pricing?

Generally, pricing isn't the biggest barrier. Meet all previous criteria, and you're likely to save money later. Some will want to sew your product before giving you a quote, and some will quote you different prices for a sample vs. production. So make sure to factor in sample cost, and know they might be different sewers doing your sample vs. production.

TO VET POTENTIAL SEWERS, ASK THE KEY QUESTIONS IN **WORKSHEET 10B.**

Emma's Story

"Know that your business will not go anywhere if you don't have a sample sewer helping you make your first prototype. This person needs to be someone you think of as your COO at this point. They're so important to you. Their feedback is crucial, their turnaround time is crucial. The way you can really impact that is with a smile. Even if you don't exactly understand what they're saying, smile and trust them. It may take a few rounds to get through to where you want your sample to be. It's going to be so much easier if you're patient with them, and with yourself too.

"Continually remind yourself that they know how to do something you don't know how to do. When you're making something for production, you want it sewn in *the most* efficient, *the most* cost-effective way. With a tailor it's going to take so much longer, and they'll set up the project in a way that doesn't have to be repeatable. But you need your product to be repeatedly sewn, efficiently, accurately every single time. A production sewer will do that for you.

"I listen to the podcast *How I Built This* a lot, and I was listening to the one about Outdoor Voices, which is an activewear company. (Hosted by Guy Raz, the show tells stories of entrepreneurs and innovators.) Outdoor Voices Founder Tyler Haney referenced that she started with a tailor in New York City, and told about her diffi-culties with it. If you want an example of someone who went that route and would not recommend it, pull up that episode."

TO FIND AND VET POTENTIAL SAMPLE SEWERS, SEE IDEAS IN **WORKSHEET 10.**

HIRE YOUR PROTOTYPE SEWER

Once you've identified your sewer, hire them! Take this oppor-tunity to be as prepared as possible. Remember, sewers are hard workers who don't have time to hold your hand and show you the way. You know your project best. Equip them for it by providing everything they need up front. Then, once your pro-totype is ready, you've reached a key milestone. At that time, you'll be ready to estimate your launch dates, which you'll read about in the next lesson.

Mentor Moment

Want Additional Help?

If you're feeling overwhelmed, you're not alone. There are many reasons why designers may need to reach out for additional help. Maybe your apparel project was supposed to be your side gig, but now it's encroaching on your main job. Maybe your timeline got crunched for reasons outside your control. Or maybe your life circumstances have changed since you started the project.

Whatever the reason, remember that the Apparel Mentor is here, should you need us. If you'd like a partner to speed your project, relieve you of some headaches, or just answer questions, visit *theapparelmentor.com*.

LESSON 11

ESTIMATE YOUR LAUNCH DATES

Lesson Objectives

In this lesson, you will:

- ▶ Celebrate your progress so far.
- ▶ Decide which path is best for estimating your launch date: full focus, life-balance, or evolving.
- ▶ Estimate two launch dates: soft launch and hard launch.
- ▶ Start planning how your role will change.

Creating apparel is a marathon, not a sprint. At times it can be hard to see the finish line. Pick your head up from the constant running. See where you're headed and appreciate where you've been. After guiding hundreds of designers through this process, I'm a believer in pushing yourself *and* slowing down enough to chart your course.

Once your prototype is sewn, you've come far enough to project two key dates: ***soft launch*** and ***hard launch***. Putting actual dates on the calendar makes everything seem real. Now you have a guidepost to keep you focused and motivated. And even though the dates will shift as your project moves forward, you'll benefit from saying your timeline out loud.

CELEBRATE YOUR PROGRESS SO FAR

If you've made your first prototype, you've reached a major milestone! You've come a long way on this journey. It's huge: You've put in a lot of hours, learned new skills, and met new people. Not only that, but you have something to show for it.

Granted, the first version is *not* your final. You'll need to make major changes before getting it right, but still—I want you to take a deep breath and celebrate how far you've come. As you'll learn in Lesson 12, this stage can be emotional for first-time designers. Not realizing that prototyping is iterative, they get disappointed upon seeing their first prototype. Changes are inevitable, and it's all part of the process.

Especially for this reason, it's time to go out to dinner and celebrate! Gather your biggest cheerleaders and take a weekend getaway. Hit the spa. Do what it takes to keep you energized for the rest of your journey.

DECIDE WHICH PATH IS RIGHT FOR YOU

Apparel designers come to the process with completely different motivations and resources. When estimating your launch date, set realistic expectations. I've provided you with three possible paths, based on the time, money, and energy you can contribute. No path is better or worse than the others. What's important is to take stock of your actual situation. Review the following descriptions and decide which best suits your lifestyle right now.

- **Full Focus:** *If you have 20 or more hours per week to dedicate to your apparel design, use this designation to* *estimate your launch date. This track also applies to you if you've engaged a full partner.*

Your clothing line will come together the fastest on this path. If this is your main priority or you've hired a partner to manage the project for you, things are going to move quicker.

- **Life-Balance:** *If you have 6 to 19 hours to devote per week, use the life-balance designation.*

  Things are still moving pretty fast on your clothing line, but it's not your full focus. Maybe you have a full-time job. Maybe you're putting in hours after the kids are in bed. Having multiple priorities can be a great place to be, but this project is going to take longer.

- **Evolve:** *If you have fewer than 5 hours a week to devote, consider yourself on the evolving track.*

  You're chipping away at this when you can, but your circumstances don't allow you to put the clothing line first. It's entirely possible to start out doing this for fun or as a hobby. Over time, your priorities may shift and allow more focus. It's not uncommon for designers to start here or waver in and out for a while.

ESTIMATE TWO LAUNCH DATES: SOFT AND HARD

WHAT'S THE DIFFERENCE?

Although you are not ready to launch yet, these dates are coming up. It's good for you to understand them first. A *soft launch* is a strategic way to get your product into the hands of a small audience, often quietly or by invitation only, to get feedback about things like price, marketing, and styling. During this phase, you will test certain elements and make tweaks before doing a full splash on a wider scale. When you get here, it isn't the time to change the *product itself,* because you are done developing it. Rather, the soft launch allows you to test *how you present it to your people.* At this stage, the manufacturer will have provided you with a few completed samples, just before they start making mass quantities. While you wait, you can do things like:

- Test your marketing and sales plan.
- Start doing photo shoots.
- Test social media channels, like Instagram.
- Bring sales samples out into the world.
- Begin wholesaling.
- Gather presales.

A *hard launch* is when you're done with manufacturing! You will then have your bulk units—one hundred, one thousand, or whatever is in your plan for your first manufacturing run. This has been your ultimate goal. You will then have actual products to sell.

ESTIMATE YOUR DATES

This lesson's worksheet features a chart that lays out the timing of the remaining steps in the process, from prototyping to hard launching your clothes! Your task is to fill in time estimates for every step in the prototyping, tech design, and manufacturing phases. In doing so, you'll reveal two important dates: soft launch and hard launch.

As you fill in your dates, have your calendar ready. You *must* cross correlate each estimated step with actual plans in your life:

- Do you have any vacations planned?
- Do you need to factor in your kids' school year or other activities?
- Is there a time of year when less gets done?
- Have you factored in holidays?
- Does your life plan involve any major personal projects like moving, helping a family member, or getting married or divorced?
- What else can you think of that will influence your timeline?

There's no way around it; life gets in the way. This isn't a bad thing, but you'll be happier and more profitable if your estimate is based in reality.

Finally, note that this timeline starts when you're getting your first prototype sewn. The first ten lessons in this book *are not* included, because there's too much variance in how long they may take different designers to complete.

Emma's Story

"Sometimes in life, the full-focus path isn't possible. Maybe you're working a full-time job, so this apparel project needs to happen during your off time and on your weekends. Or maybe you have kids and that's your main focus. After they go to bed, you're putting in hours for your line. The life-balance path can be a great place to be, but just know that it does take longer.

"I started in the evolve section. You know, it was definitely a hobby, and I was doing it for fun. And then it turned into more of my lifestyle. I was putting a lot more time into it, but still working a full-time job always. I wasn't really sure which way I was gonna go. Was I going to stay working in the apparel industry? I wasn't yet sure I wanted to go and launch this brand all on its own. And then I did eventually end up quitting corporate. I decided it was worth my full focus, so I started putting in 40 hours a week on it. So, yeah, I've taken all the paths, at different times. I have seen firsthand how much faster it moves when you put in more time. And yet I know from personal experience, that full focus wasn't an option for me right away.

"When setting your launch date, make sure it works for your product and your life. I think it's really important to cross reference these dates with your personal calendar. Do you have trips coming up that will push things back? Or birthdays or surgeries or gosh, who knows what? Things will always be in flux. Maybe you can put this chart into an Excel document that you can constantly go back and update.

"Keep in mind that your first time through you're not gonna know exactly how your partners perform. You're not gonna know they're kind of always running a little bit behind. Or, if you're like me, you may fail to predict that your order will get caught up in Chinese New Year and take twelve weeks, not six. So yeah, definitely pad your launch date. And remember to have fun with it."

WHAT IS YOUR ESTIMATED LAUNCH DATE? REMEMBER DEVELOPING PRODUCT TAKES A BIT LONGER THAN MOST PEOPLE EXPECT! TO ESTIMATE YOUR LAUNCH DATES, COMPLETE THE CHART ON **WORKSHEET 11.**

START PLANNING HOW YOUR ROLE WILL CHANGE

As soon as you reach soft launch, your role as business owner will change immensely. This can be a rocky transition if you're not prepared. After spending anywhere from a year to several years designing and developing your product line, your focus shifts entirely once it's on the market.

As you'll recall from the introduction to this book, I make the case that your job as a clothing designer and project manager includes three main prongs:

- Making apparel
- Marketing and sales
- Running business operations

This book covers the first of these. Once you hit your soft launch, you'll be transitioning to the marketing and selling role. It's never too soon to start thinking about what this will look like for you. And of course, you'll need to be running effective business operations throughout.

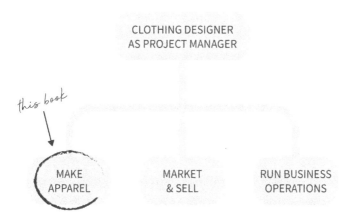

Let's review what this may mean for you. If you're reading this book in preparation for starting a line down the road, you now have a much better understanding of what to expect. Keep dreaming and taking steps as you can. Even small actions add up, over time.

On the other hand, let's assume you've followed the lessons so far. Assuming you've made the first version of your prototype, consider the following estimates:

- If you're on the *full-focus* path, you can expect to hit your soft launch date in about five months.
- If you're on the *life-balance* path, you can expect to hit your soft launch date in about ten months.
- If you're on the *evolve* path, you can expect to hit your soft launch date in about twenty months.

UPDATE YOUR CHART AS YOU GO

Keep blank copies of **Worksheet 11** handy. As your project moves forward, there are many things that can cause these dates to change. As you complete each step, fill in *actual dates* and update your remaining estimates accordingly.

LESSON 12

EVALUATE YOUR FIRST PROTOTYPE

Lesson Objectives

In this lesson, you will:

- ► Adopt a resilient mindset for the prototype process.
- ► Evaluate your first prototype for fit.
- ► Evaluate your first prototype for washability.
- ► Gather feedback and engage vendors as needed—fabric mill, patternmaker, and/or sewer.

Now that you have set your launch dates, it's time to get back to your prototyping. If there's one thing to know about prototypes, it's this: Prepare yourself for iterations, because this is a *process*. The most common pitfall for new designers is that they rush prototyping, thinking it'll be quick and easy. I've seen people in tears after seeing their first sewn version. If only they'd known that imperfect versions are normal and even needed.

ADOPT A RESILIENT MINDSET

When your first prototype arrives, you get to see your design in real life for the first time. This is an exciting milestone, especially if you've been dreaming of your garment for awhile. But for many designers, the fun can feel short lived. Many factors go into producing a garment, and this is the stage where problems get revealed.

Car makers don't get it right on their first prototype, and neither will you. For that matter, any creative endeavor requires an evolution. Novels require multiple drafts, and films look nothing like the raw footage shot in the beginning. Save yourself some stress and accept that your first prototype will need fixing.

— — Mentor Moment — —

I've talked about this already, I know, but it bears repeating: manufacturing good-quality clothing items requires *so much expertise* in so many different ways. The industry often tends to diminish the value of the work with the words they use; pattern-makers are really *pattern engineers*, you know, because the sheer amount of math and physics that goes into this work is truly astonishing. On that note, when I first got started, it was interesting (and infuriating) to see that people balked at the prices I was charging. (I was charging *maybe* a quarter of what I should have, of what we were worth, for reference.)

It really lit my feminist fire, because in most traditional men's industries, people have no problem paying thousands of dollars and going through dozens of iterations to produce a good product. Build a car or shoot a movie and that's the norm. But suddenly you're designing a jacket and you want to pay $20 for development and you expect it to be perfect on the first try? Give me a break.

I know I'm probably preaching to the choir at this point, but I want you to remember how much value there is in the work you're doing and how much work it takes to get things right. Don't be disappointed when you need many iterations for your prototyping to work out. That's just part of the process. That's how it works. Remind yourself that you're in a complicated business, and you're producing something of tremendous value. Use the proper terminology. Approach your work with confidence. Don't be hesitant about asking your collaborators and vendors and prototype designers for more input and time. The people that understand the development process know that this is an expensive and lengthy step—and that it's crucial for making something worthwhile.

While you're evaluating your prototype, remember this too. There are a surprising number of factors that go into developing a garment. Any one of them can go wrong, and in a first prototype, many do. In this lesson, you'll evaluate several factors for your base size, including materials, fit, design, and washability. Then you'll organize the feedback and submit it to the vendors who'll help you tweak your next version.

Instead of getting upset, look at flaws as your chance to improve the garment. Evaluate each as a scientist would, with curiosity about how to improve the next version. Each imperfection was caused by something. Maybe the pattern is off slightly. Maybe the fabric is the wrong weight or stretchiness. Or perhaps your sewer used the wrong thread or tension. You'll want to gather the right group of trusted advisors, who know the industry and can solve these little mysteries with you.

EVALUATE FIT

When it comes to evaluating your prototype, there are two main categories: fit and washability. Let's start with fit. As I've said before, fit is everything. It makes or breaks your garment. To evaluate yours, you need to see how it looks, feels, and functions on an actual human being. When it comes to fit, there are three main things that can influence it: design, sewing, and materials.

Once you identify a problem, there's someone who's best suited to fix it. Generally, a patternmaker fixes design, a sewer fixes sewing issues, and a vendor can provide you with different fabric or trims. In this lesson, your job is to identify the problems and document them. Then, in the next lesson, you'll engage vendors to fix them.

STEP 1: IDENTIFY YOUR FIT MODEL

To prepare for your fitting, decide who will be involved. First, who will serve as your fit model? For this, find someone whose measurements represent your ideal client. Ideally, they should be easy to work with, and game for being part of this experimental phase. It's okay to choose yourself, but remember: This is not an opportunity to make a custom garment for yourself; your role is to represent the needs of others like you.

STEP 2: HAND PICK YOUR TRUSTED TEAM

You need to hand select a small team of advisors to be involved. This is not the time for widespread show and tell. (Don't plan a launch party or plan a photoshoot just yet.) Most people don't get what a prototype is for. They'll expect a final version and won't respond well at this stage. This can backfire by planting unnecessary doubts in your mind. So, be selective. Show your work only to those who know the industry and/or have the ability to view the prototype objectively, with expertise.

I recommend recruiting some sort of professional who is used to fitting garments. The more specific their feedback is, the better. It's also a good idea to get feedback from someone in your target market, someone who shares the qualities you outline for your ideal client. The good news is that this meeting does not have to happen in person. When selecting your team, the most important thing is to find people with industry knowledge and objectivity. When I've seen new designers get into trouble at this stage, it's because they asked for feedback from friends and family. As well meaning as they may be, don't get them involved. Chances are they don't know what to look for, they understand your market, or both.

STEP 3: CONDUCT THE FITTING

Arrange a time for your model to wear the prototype, with as many people from your team involved as possible. Remember, the fit model can be you or someone close to you. The absolute best-case scenario is to arrange a in-person meeting where everyone can view the model from all sides. That said, this isn't always possible, and that's okay. At Clothier Design Source, we've conducted plenty of fittings through video or photos.

Regardless of who's in the room, however, you must have a camera with you! A key part of the fitting is taking photos (and/or video), for use in later conversations. During the fitting, look at the garment from the front, side, and back. View the model from each angle, one at a time, and take thorough notes. Write down what you like, and especially what you don't. Have each person involved record their thoughts. (Later, you'll compile them into a cohesive document.)

Answer Questions

Be prepared with a reliable way to take notes. Do what works for you: Fill out this lesson's worksheet, bring your own notebook, or record your thoughts on a handy device. Do what works for you, in a way that you can keep track easily later on. If you don't stay organized now, you'll kill yourself later, through a death of a thousand cuts.

Answer these questions:

- Does the garment hang the way you hoped it would?
- Does it look and feel right, in the right places on the body?
- Does anything seem off? Does it feel right when moving?
- What might be causing this problem? Design? Materials? Sewing?
- Which vendor might be the best person to fix it? Patternmaker? Sewer? Vendor?

Even if you don't have sewing experience, it's okay to use layman's terms. You still have eyes, and you can sense when something isn't right. Describe it how you see it. And lean on your experienced team members for more specifics.

Take Photos and Troubleshoot Problems

After the fitting, you'll conduct conversations with vendors whose job it is to fix the problems, namely your patternmaker and sewer. They'll need to see what you're talking about. So, think of your fitting as your one shining opportunity to capture

Note: Every project is different, so it's up to you to decide how many sizes to launch. On average, offering five sizes makes the most sense for widespread appeal.

YIELD: WHAT IT IS AND WHY IT MATTERS

If you've taken beginner sewing, you may recall there's a trick to cutting fabric. If you've never sewn in your life, know this: Cutting requires technique, and doing it wrong is costly. Specifically, you want to do it in a way that yields the most fabric. As such, "yield" refers to the amount of fabric you'll use per garment, on average. Fabric is money, so you must pay attention to this number.

Several factors determine yield for an apparel project. For instance, bigger sizes yield more fabric. But garment size is only part of the equation. Another huge factor in determining yield is pattern placement. To cut, a vendor positions patterns on the fabric, then cuts around them. Patterns placed strategically yield fabric effectively. In other words, proper arrangement prevents needless waste.

Most of the time, brands manufacture multiple garments at a time, often using the same fabric on more than one item. Imagine what a difference it would make to have a specialist placing all these patterns together in an engineered way, rather than throwing them down carelessly. This process of precise arrangement requires a specialist called a marker maker, who has high-level skills.

MAXIMIZING FABRIC

Look at this diagram. It shows how tank-top patterns might be laid out to yield fabric strategically. (Each shade represents a different size.) At first glance, this may look simple. But a marker maker knows better. Their job is to find the absolute most efficient combination of the pieces involved. Your job is to treat your factory well, being grateful that you don't need to have their knowledge, which covers math, construction, computer literacy, problem-solving, and industrial diagnostics.

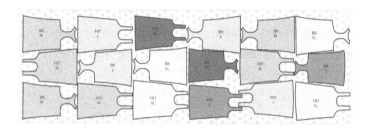

HOW YOU'LL USE YIELD

Though you don't need to know the ins and outs of marker making, you absolutely *do need to know your yield.* The amount of fabric used per piece will tell you a lot about how much your project will cost, and how much fabric to order for future batches.

Unfortunately, yield can't be calculated accurately until after manufacturing. This figure is entirely dependent on which styles you produce in a given run, and how many sizes. Because this combination tends to vary each time a designer goes to the factory, this number will vary too. That said, you can and should produce yield estimates as soon as you can.

The best way to do this is to ask your patternmaker. When you hire them to grade your patterns, you'll instruct them to estimate your yield. Although the final yield can't be known until after manufacturing, the patternmaker's estimate will help you forecast your budget.